A Simple Faith

A Simple Faith

Insights for Living in a Complex World

Fletcher Spruce
Compiled by James R. Spruce

Beacon Hill Press of Kansas City
Kansas City, Missouri

ISBN: 083-411-626X

Printed in the
United States of America

Cover Design: Mike Walsh

Unless otherwise indicated, all Scripture quotations are from the King James Version.

The following versions are also quoted:

Library of Congress Cataloging-in-Publication Data

Spruce, Fletcher.
    A simple faith : insights for living in a complex world / Fletcher
Spruce ; compiled by James R. Spruce.
        p.   cm.
    Collection of essays and stories originally published in Standard
from 1959-1975.
    ISBN 0-8341-1626-X (pbk.)
    1. Meditations.   2. Christian life—Nazarene authors.   I. Spruce,
James R.   II. Title.
BV4832.2.S75   1997
242—dc21   96-39977
                                                                    CIP

10   9   8   7   6   5   4   3   2   1

For Mother and Sallye

CONTENTS

Cultivating a Christian Family

Finding Faith in Well-known Characters

Foreword

Fueling Faith Across Generations

Every generation produces spiritual giants who are largely unknown to future generations. Fletcher Spruce was one of those quiet giants of his time who is almost unknown to the present generation.

Often spiritually robust folks from past eras remain strangers to new generations because nobody thinks to tell their stories. No one celebrates what they did or publishes what they wrote. Sometimes it seems like creative faith has to be reinvented anew by each generation. But for those of us who try to write, we frequently find that ideas that seem incredibly new to us have been around for years, long before anyone thought about our being on planet Earth. *A Simple Faith* is like that; it will make you think wonderful new-old thoughts.

Just now a tiny glimmer of faith being passed across generations seems to be happening in the contemporary church. In some places, the family of God views itself like an extended human family so children, parents, and grandparents share common, life-transforming, intergenerational faith. That's what *A Simple Faith* tries to do. Every page opens another timeless insight for serious pilgrims—Xers, boomers, seniors, and those who fit none of these categories. The father/son writers are stalwart examples of vibrant faith reaching from one generation to the next.

Fletcher Spruce, the father, ministered by preaching, writing, and providing administrative leadership to the Church of the Nazarene. Though he effectively served in every assignment, he was especially loved as a great soul. He was a quality person who lived what he wrote.

James Spruce, the son, now in the prime of his ministry, follows in his father's footsteps as pastor, writer, and church administrator. I knew and loved the father, and I know and love the son. I am better, nobler, and more Christlike for knowing them both. Jim has honored me by his request that I write this introduction.

Memories from long ago bring back sunny, spiritual Sunday afternoons when we read the take-home Sunday School papers. Quiet Sabbaths offered a good time to read, and I cherished the terse, imaginative writings of Fletcher Spruce. For years, he wrote a weekly short essay in the *Standard*, an adult Sunday School paper, and the essays were well read. He also wrote books—always with flair and a magnetic call to satisfying faith. Now his son James is publishing too.

I recommend *A Simple Faith* as a stimulus for serious spiritual adventure. Son James Spruce and editor Gay Leonard have provided a wonderful contemporary edit to these pithy essays. These five-minute reads will help shape you into Christlikeness, and that will satisfy your soul.

Try sharing these ideas across generations with your children or your parents. From personal experience I know it can be a rich experience. Let me explain. I recall what these writings did to me and will keep doing as I keep this book handy near my Bible and hymnbook. I know how it impacted my mother; a little while ago I asked her if she remembered Fletcher Spruce's writings. With a spiritual zest she answered, "Do I remember! I even have a scrapbook of those writings." I was also encouraged to believe these faith lessons will work across generations when I heard how a publishing focus group representing several ages read the material with relish.

Perhaps the Lord will use *A Simple Faith* to raise up Xers and boomers to do some great Kingdom work like He did through Fletcher and is doing through James. I pray it will be so. You may be the one God will use.

—*Neil B. Wiseman*

Preface

This collection of essays and stories, published originally in *Standard*, reflects the heart and soul of their author and my dad, Fletcher Spruce.

These short pieces are timeless. They reveal the memories of a little boy on his father's farm south of San Antonio long before the Great Depression. They recall the hopes and dreams a pastor had for his church. They call broken people to faith, indifferent people to service, and all of us to commitment. They are at once bold and folksy, ancient and fresh, pointed and fair. Through the lens of the Scriptures, Dad gives colorful word pictures of Bible characters and themes. You get the impression that God is a God of high expectation. You also get the feeling that God is a Father waiting on the front porch for His children to come home.

My sister, Sara, and I are thankful for a mom and dad who took time to love and nurture us as well as serve the church. Both of us are especially appreciative to Mother for her ministries of compassion at home, which gave Dad time to write.

I wish to thank our office secretaries, Cathey Galvas and Julie Chenault, and Tammy Rice, reader, for their assistance with this project.

Pastor's Study
Flint Central

Knowing God the Father, Jesus the Son, and the Holy Spirit

O Lord, Our Lord, How Majestic ...

Scripture: "Great is the LORD and most worthy of praise;
his greatness no one can fathom."

(Ps. 145:3, NIV)

◆ *God is all-wise.* He sits in the library of His infinite wisdom,
all knowledge at His command. He knows the past because it has already happened. He knows the future because it is going to happen.
God makes no mistakes. He never blunders blindly. He is never
caught off guard.

◆ *God is all-powerful.* He stands within the engine room of His
infinite power, all ability within His grasp. There is nothing impossible with Him. He who flung the stars from His fingertips into their
place and set them in clocklike regularity, He who fashioned a man
from the moist clay and breathed into him the breath of life and
made him a living soul, this same all-powerful God pressed energy
into the invisible atom—and He controls all of it.

◆ *God is everywhere.* He has fashioned for himself a limitless
garden called space and has strewn the paths of it with the glittering
dust of a thousand Milky Ways, each of which is a thousand solar
systems more spacious than our own. Its immensity staggers us. But
when we remember that the Creator is greater than the sum total of
all His creations, its size comforts us, for God fills all He has created.
His everywhereness is described by the writer who said when he
soared to the highest heaven, God was there; when he descended into
the blackest hell, God was there.

But God is neither too big nor too busy to forget me. His love
and His holiness fill my heart, dispelling all my sins and supplying
all my needs. "How great Thou art!"

Prayer: *O Lord, I cannot comprehend Your greatness. I do not
deserve Your great love. But I thank You for both.*

The Ultimate Description of God

Scripture: "For God so loved the world that he gave his only begotten Son, that whosoever believeth in him might not perish, but have everlasting life."

(John 3:16)

"The proof of God's amazing love is this: that it was *while we were sinners* that Christ died for us" (Rom. 5:8, PHILLIPS, emphasis added).

◆ *God is love.* Love is not simply a part of His nature. It *is* His nature. Love is not only one of His attributes; it is the essence of His being. The moral law is love speaking in holiness. The natural law is love displayed in order. Love is the ultimate description of God.

◆ *God loves sinners.* Not sin, but sinners. God hates, abhors, detests, and despises sin. But God loves sinners, even though they are corrupt and evil. Jesus always had compassion on sinners. He was quick to forgive the woman taken in adultery, the woman at Jacob's Well, and the woman who had seven devils. His love is equally tender, deep, and boundless today.

◆ *God's love is expensive.* A patriot will give his life for his country. A parent will pay high ransom for the safe return of a captured child. But God's love is more expensive than that. It is love for an enemy. Christ died for His enemies, praying, "Father, forgive them; for they know not what they do" (Luke 23:34). This divine love for sinners is God's unspeakable gift. Where else in all history is to be found a description of such expensive love? So exquisitely valuable is this unparalleled redemptive love of God that it alone makes the evil holy, the impure clean, the guilty pardoned, and imprisoned free.

Prayer: *O Lord, accept my repentance for all sin. Forgive my every wayward act and attitude and make me Your child.*

God Is...

Scripture: "God is spirit" (John 4:24).
"God is faithful" (1 Cor. 10:13).
"God is light" (1 John 1:5). "God is love" (4:16, all NIV).

What is God like? He does not have a body, for He is Spirit. But the devil is also a spirit. So are the angels. So are we. What kind of Spirit is God?

He is an infinite Spirit, boundless, immeasurable, without limit of time, space, or degree. He is everywhere at the same time, filling all space and all things with His presence. He is self-existent without beginning. He is eternal without ending. He is ceaseless activity, yet He never changes. He is pure and perfect. He is the First Cause, the Creator of all things. He is infinite in wisdom. He is all-good and all-powerful. He is a loving Spirit. Indeed, God is a *holy* Spirit, not able to tolerate sin without a remedy.

That remedy He provided at Calvary! Humanity fell into Satan's clutches, but God clothed himself with flesh in the form of His own Son and came to bleed and die as God-Man, making atonement for sin.

And having provided redemption for every member of the fallen race, God continues actively seeking them with His Spirit—convicting, convincing, persuading.

As the redeemed of God worship Him, they recognize a fellowship of kindred spirits. God made humanity in His own image, so that we may fellowship with Him. Though we cannot shake hands with God, we can commune with Him. We do not worship an image of Him, for there is no image of God except the "image of the invisible," His Son, Jesus Christ, our Lord and Savior. But we "walk in the spirit" in communion, in adoration, and in fellowship. His Spirit "beareth witness with our spirit."

Prayer: *God, You are many more things than we can imagine, but thank You for being all we know You to be.*

No Wonder They Call Him "Wonderful"

Scripture: ". . . and this the title that he bears—'A wonder of a counsellor, a divine hero, a father for all time, a peaceful prince!'"

(Isa. 9:6, MOFFATT)

◆ *Jesus was wonderful in His birth.* Prophecy pointed to it. He was conceived of the Holy Spirit in a virgin. Many angelic manifestations attended His earthly appearance. How wonderful was His birth!

◆ *He was wonderful in His nature.* Both man and God, both human and divine, He was two complete and entire natures wrapped into one Person. He was as divine as if He had never been human, and as human as if He had never been divine. "In him dwelleth all the fulness of the Godhead bodily," wrote Paul to the Colossians (2:9).

◆ *He was wonderful in His personality.* Although He never advertised, He is the best-known figure in human history. Although He never journeyed far from His birthplace, millions have traveled to see where He lived and died. Although He was not born in a palace, kings have bowed before Him. Although not schooled in the great universities, His words hung heavy with wisdom that mystifies scholars still today. Although a poor man, the wealth of millions has been made available to promote His gospel.

◆ *He was wonderful in His words.* He made claims for himself that no other person ever dared make. He made commands to His followers that no officer could expect of his soldiers. He made promises to all Christians that none other could possibly fulfill. He made invitations to the needy that no other person would think of making.

◆ *He was wonderful in His death.* Jesus died—not like a martyr for a lost cause, not like a patriot for His country, not like a victim of His own devices. He died as only the God-Man could die: redemptively, vicariously, and sacrificially. He became victorious over death itself!

Prayer: *Thank You, God, that You named Your Son with all the right names. He is wonderful!*

What Is Jesus Like?

Scripture: "For in Christ all the fullness of the Deity
lives in bodily form."

(Col. 2:9, NIV)

The Bible tells us much about what Jesus is like:

◆ *He is eternal.* He existed before the worlds were created, for He had a hand in their creation. He will never cease to exist.

◆ *He is divine.* He is God, a member of the Trinity. He is as divine as if He had never become a human being.

◆ *He was human.* He was as much a human being as if He had never been divine. He was two complete, whole natures in one, the God-Man.

◆ *He was divinely conceived* of the Holy Ghost and born of the Virgin Mary. His mother was a human being; His Father was God.

◆ He died not as a martyr, not as a misunderstood fanatic, but vicariously, paying the price for the redemption of the human race. *He died to save us from our sins.*

◆ *He arose from the tomb, conquering death.* The angel who rolled the stone away did not awake Him from death. Nor did the angel roll away the stone to let Him out of the tomb. Jesus was already risen from the grave before the stone was rolled away. His resurrection was an essential part of the plan to redeem us.

◆ *He ascended into heaven.* He is there making intercession for us with the Father.

◆ *He is coming soon.* This is His promise, and the signs of His coming are being fulfilled. He could return today.

◆ *He demands some things of the sinner:* a complete repentance, a turning from sin, a new birth, a perfect obedience.

◆ *He demands some things of His followers:* that we live holy, pure lives; that we be faithful in our service; that we tell this blessed story everywhere and constantly until He comes again.

Prayer: *Dear Jesus, we thank You for representing our Heavenly Father in mortal flesh. We honor You today.*

Christ the King

Scripture: "Mary Magdalene went to the disciples with the news: 'I have seen the Lord!'"

(John 20:18, NIV)

Christ lacked the common qualities of earthly kings. He could not claim kingship on the basis of appearance, for "he hath no form nor comeliness . . . there is no beauty" (Isa. 53:2); not in success, for "he is despised and rejected" (v. 3); not in reputation, for "he shall be called a Nazarene" (Matt. 2:23); not in riches, for He "hath not where to lay his head" (8:20); not in rank, for He was called the carpenter's son; not in demeanor, for He washed His disciples' feet. His kingdom was not of this world. His throne was a cross, His crown was of thorns, His scepter was a reed, His royal robe was borrowed briefly. They mocked Him and crucified Him. They would have "no king but Caesar."

But Christ *is* King! His kingdom is within us. He rules not with legions, but with love . . . not with guns, but with grace . . . not with bombs, but with blessings. His is the Sword of the Spirit, which saves rather than kills, which cleanses rather than cremates. His throne is the human heart. His scepter is the yielded will. His crown is our complete consecration. Christ is our King, and His banner over us is love.

The claims of His kingdom are broad: (1) The world is His because He created it. As King, Christ is at the controls of the universe. (2) The race is His because He ransomed it. Satan's dominion is now broken in millions of happy hearts because Jesus is King. Therefore we are able to sing:

"With Jesus, my Savior,
I'm a child of the King!"

Prayer: *Thank You, God, for Your kingship in my life.*

The Voice of the Vacant Tomb

Scripture: "They have taken the Lord out of the tomb, and we don't know where they have put him!"

(John 20:2, NIV)

Have you ever turned the dial of your radio or flipped through the channels of your television late at night, trying to keep count of the voices appealing for your attention? So it is in all life. The world, the flesh, the devil, things fundamental and trivial—they all clamor to be heard. But one voice rings out clear and strong above all others: the voice of the empty tomb.

◆ *It is an eloquent voice.* The empty tomb speaks of a Christ who died but conquered death itself. The last enemy is destroyed, and the sting of death has lost its poison. The empty tomb speaks of armed guards keeping watch over a dead Man, yet unable to keep Him dead. It speaks of the weakness of the seal of the Roman Empire when the mortal puts on immortality.

◆ *It is an assuring voice.* The empty tomb tells us that our faith in Christ is not in vain, for He is not dead. It tells us that our fears are unfounded, for ours is a living Savior. It tells us that doubting disciples can explore the wounds opened especially for them and fall at His pierced feet crying, "My Lord and my God."

◆ *It is a hopeful voice.* The empty tomb shouts that sinners can be forgiven, that carnality can be cleansed, that the holy life can become a reality. It speaks of a glad reunion in God's tomorrow where we shall fellowship eternally with those whom we have loved.

◆ *It is a compelling voice.* The empty tomb commands us to witness to what we know to be true. It tells us that ours is a gospel of power if released, but a gospel of weakness if kept silent. It tells us that others are waiting to hear from our lips a personal witness of His resurrection.

Prayer: *God, You spoke loudly on Mount Sinai with Moses and again through a baby's cry from the womb of a virgin. But nothing thundered like the silence of Christ's empty tomb.*

God's Perfect Gift

Scripture: "Wait for the gift my Father promised."
(Acts 1:4, NIV)

◆ *The Holy Spirit is a Gift* . . . the gift of a Person, not a thing. He is God's Gift. He cannot be bought with money or earned by deeds.

◆ *The Holy Spirit is a conditional Gift.* Only born-again Christians may receive Him. Only those who earnestly desire more of the fullness of God may receive Him. Only those who are walking in the light and love of God may receive Him. This Gift of the Holy Spirit is for everyone, but each one must qualify.

◆ *The Holy Spirit is a Gift every Christian needs.* Beyond repentance and regeneration is the Upper Room blessing and power for service. To His disciples Jesus said, "Tarry . . . until ye be endued with power from on high" (Luke 24:49); "Wait for the promise of the Father" (Acts 1:4); "Ye shall receive power, after that the Holy Ghost is come upon you" (v. 8).

◆ *The Holy Spirit is a Gift whom God earnestly desires to give to His children.* "This is the will of God, even your sanctification" (1 Thess. 4:3); "Be ye holy; for I am holy" (1 Pet. 1:16); "Receive ye the Holy Ghost" (John 20:22). God knows the needs of His children. He knows that we need His Spirit within us to give us power for service, victory in temptation, and joy in our hours of heaviness.

◆ *The Holy Spirit is a Gift that you, as a child of God, may receive now.* Do not wait at all to receive Him. If you know that your sins are forgiven, you sense your need for His Spirit. Simply surrender everything to Him and by faith invite Him in His fullness, His cleansing, and His power for service. "They were all filled with the Holy Ghost."

Prayer: *Thank You, Lord, for reminding us to be steadfast in our walk with You while we await the assurance of a personal relationship with the Holy Spirit.*

Keeping His Promise

Scripture: "The world cannot accept him, because it neither sees him nor knows him."

(John 14:17, NIV)

"Another Comforter" was the promise of Christ. Although He was going away, He promised the disciples that they would not be left as spiritual orphans. The Father would send this other "Comforter, which is the Holy Ghost" (John 14:26).

Notice to whom the Holy Spirit would be sent: to those who love Him. And what is the evidence that we love Jesus? We keep His commandments. Our Lord said, "If ye love me, keep my commandments. . . . And . . . the Father . . . shall give you another Comforter . . . whom the world cannot receive" (vv. 15-17). The person of the world is not a candidate for holiness. This experience is for those who are saved, who love God, who keep His commandments.

Here is a definite promise, a distinct promise that Jesus and His Father (Acts 1:4) made to His disciples. It is the promise of the Comforter, the Holy Ghost, the Holy Spirit, the Spirit of Truth. No promise in all the Bible is noted with a greater simplicity, certainty, and urgency.

Like other promises in the Bible, this one is conditional. It is made only to those who will meet the conditions laid down within the framework of the promise. The Holy Spirit is promised to the Christians, the saved ones, the obedient ones, to those who love Him and keep His commandments.

Like other promises in the Bible, this one has been and is being fulfilled wherever and whenever the conditions are met. The first great moment in history making the fulfillment of this promise was Pentecost. Again and again since that historic day, the Holy Spirit has come into the hearts and lives of all who have met God's conditions. The results are thrilling beyond utterance! "Have ye received the Holy Ghost since you believed?" (Acts 19:2).

Prayer: *God, we want to walk with You in obedience so we may know You in truth.*

Supernatural Assistance

Scripture: "When he comes, he will convict the world of
guilt. . . . The Spirit . . . will guide you into all truth."
(John 16:8, 13, NIV)

It is absolutely impossible for us to become mature Christians in our
own strength and by our own self-discipline. We must have the help of the
Holy Spirit. Without that help, we become self-made instead of God-made.

The world has plenty of dismal examples of self-made persons.
But with the help of the Holy Spirit, it is gloriously possible for us to
develop and mature into abundant Christlikeness. Here are some of
the ways the Holy Spirit helps us.

◆　*He fills* us with himself. With the sinful condition of the
human personality cleansed, we are ready for growth in the Spirit.

◆　*He enables* and empowers us to overcome—to cope—to be
victorious. We cannot accomplish this in our own strength.

◆　*He motivates* and energizes us to achieve and accomplish.
He gives a holy enthusiasm to do what God wants done.

◆　*He rebukes* and warns us when we say or do something that
ought not to be said or done.

◆　*He teaches* and instructs us in our search for new truths and
new light. If we are sensitive, He will help us learn the ways of the Spirit.

◆　*He guides* and directs. Even when we cannot see the path
clearly, He leads us into all truth.

◆　*He refreshes* and renews us so that we will not faint by the
way. He keeps us ever fresh and anointed with His Spirit.

Let us rejoice with Lucy J. Rider, who sang . . .
Child of the Kingdom, be filled with the Spirit!
Nothing but fullness thy longing can meet;
'Tis the enduement for life and for service.
Thine is the promise so certain, so sweet!

Prayer: *Holy Spirit, I thank You for convicting me of sin and then
for leading me into all truth. You are faithful!*

Changed Forever

Scripture: "Then Peter said, 'Silver or gold I do not have, but . . . in the name of Jesus Christ of Nazareth, walk.'"
(Acts 3:6, NIV)

On this certain day soon after Pentecost, things were fairly routine again in Jerusalem. Peter and John were on their way to the Temple to pray at 3 P.M. The social welfare workers laid the lame man there by the gate Beautiful to beg.

The Temple was the same. The beggar was the same. But Peter and John were different. The afterglow of their Pentecost experience lingered and gleamed in their hearts. They were looking for opportunities to witness and to share the newfound power of the Holy Spirit in their lives. Their chance came when they saw the lame man at the gate. They noticed him for the first time. It was strange that they had not seen him before, for he had been there for years. But the by-products of Pentecost were beginning to show through. The fullness of the Holy Spirit did not increase their opportunities. It opened their eyes. It warmed their sympathies. It enlarged their vision. It made them see the worth of forgotten individuals. It helped them recognize the potential wrapped up even in the most helpless cases.

The Holy Spirit had also placed the by-product of faith in the hearts of Peter and John. They believed the lame man could be made whole and that they could be God's instruments to bring this to pass. Before the Day of Pentecost they were spectators while Christ did the miracles. But now they were themselves walking miracles because the Spirit dwelt in them.

Another by-product was fellowship. Peter and John did not have much in common before they were filled with the Holy Spirit. The gap in their ages and the difference in their temperaments kept them a little apart. But now there was a common bond of the Spirit that made them closer than brothers.

It is God's good pleasure to give you His Holy Spirit with all its blessed by-products.

Prayer: *Lord, though I may not preach like Peter or heal like John, Your Spirit provides many good by-products in my life for which I am thankful.*

Reining in Our Relationships with God and Others

Getting Along When You'd Rather Just Go Away

Scripture: "So in irritation they parted company."
(Acts 15:39, MOFFATT)

◆ Differences are inevitable. God made us different. He expects us to see things differently and to say so.

◆ Differences are necessary in a free society. The minority voice must be heard; the opposition must be respected.

◆ It is natural for Christians to differ where God is silent. God is silent in the details of nonessentials, like what color to paint the church nursery.

◆ Christians have a right to disagree. But they have no right to disagree in an unholy manner.

◆ Excessive emotional demonstration is never the path to a harmonious solution. Christians should be courteous, kind, and charitable, even when it takes self-control.

◆ Christian harmony is possible only when we are willing and determined to have it. This may involve a careful examination of our motives and values.

◆ Differences that drift or explode into dissension grieve God and hurt innocent people. It is a tragic thing to see someone constantly digging up the old hatchet for another bloodletting. God and time are the best healers.

◆ Disharmony is generally directly attributable to a self-seeking spirit on the part of at least one person. We should each take care that we never fit that description.

◆ About 99 percent of the things we fight about are not worth fighting about. Let's work together to produce harmony and unity.

Prayer: *God, make us big enough to admit our differences and find reconciliation.*

Taking It On the Chin

Scripture: "If we are thrown into the . . . furnace, . . . God is able to save us . . . But even if he does not, . . . we will not serve your gods."

(Dan. 3:17-18, NIV)

When you seem to be at an impasse with your enemies, what is the proper Christian response?

◆ *Compromise if you should.* Is the issue vital? Is it worth dying for? A driver's stubborn refusal to move just a few inches can cause a terrible accident. There are times when it is good to give in a bit.

◆ *Don't compromise if you shouldn't.* There are times when compromising is sin, when giving even an inch is wrong. In times like these, it is better to be thrown into the fiery furnace or the lions' den than to compromise. It is better to lose your so-called "friends" than it is to lose your soul. In life's "give-me-liberty-or-give-me-death" experiences, there can be no choice. With Martin Luther we must say, "Here I stand. I can do no other. So help me God." Christ refused compromise, even though it meant embracing death.

◆ *Keep Christlike attitudes.* Almost anyone can be sweet when all is going well. But the real test comes with the cutting word, the icy stare, or the cynical blast. What is your attitude toward your enemies? Christ's instructions to turn the other cheek and to go the second mile are not messages of weakness. Only the power of an inner grace gives spiritual composure in the face of Satan's fiercest hostility.

◆ *Seek ways to win your enemies.* This is not always possible. Christ sought to win His enemies, and they nailed Him to a cross. But His cross has become earth's most compelling pulpit, and millions believe! Face your enemies with love, even though they crush you. Love is of God.

Prayer: *God, help me never give up, give in, or give out when Your will is at stake.*

Melody or Harmony?

Scripture: "So the churches were strengthened in the faith and grew daily in numbers."

(Acts 16:5, NIV)

Paul and Barnabas, partners in the gospel, eventually parted company. Their experience together as well as their parting teaches Christians important lessons about how we work together within the church.

◆ *Good people have a right to differ* (Acts 15:39-41). Paul and Barnabas disagreed over John Mark—so strongly, in fact, that each man went his separate way. In our humanity, we will see things differently. God can help us to disagree in an agreeable manner.

◆ *Big people are willing to admit they are wrong.* Paul did. Years later, he reenlisted John Mark, who was profitable in the ministry (2 Tim. 4:11). Either Paul had changed, or Mark had changed. Perhaps both. Whatever had happened to make the difference, Paul used his reverse gears. God will bless the person who has the grace and humility to admit that he has been wrong.

◆ *Worthy leadership reproduces itself* (Acts 16:3). Paul's leadership was perpetuated in young Timothy. He was spiritually challenged by the great apostle. Every Christian worker, teacher, and pastor should strive to train new leaders.

◆ *Wise people respect the collective conscience of holy leaders* (Acts 16:4). Paul respected the judgment of these holy leaders and published the good word everywhere. Harmony comes when we respect the decisions of our church leaders.

◆ *Sincere people insist on divine leadership* (Acts 16:6-10). Paul insisted on knowing God's direction; he refused to make a move without it. We must consider God's will first in every choice, decision, and action.

Prayer: *Father, help my church grow in spite of individual personalities, including my own.*

Peaceful Strokes for Differing Folks

Scripture: "Don't criticise people, and you will not be criticised." (Matt. 7:1, PHILLIPS)

Christians do not always agree. Peter and Paul differed. Barnabas and Paul differed. You and I differ. God made us different, and He expects us to see things differently. But we must keep our disagreements on the agreeable level and never let them degenerate into carnal arguments or fights. How can this be done?

◆ Pray that God will keep your motives pure and sweet.

◆ Never sit in judgment of your opposition (Matt. 7:1-2).

◆ Do not jump to your own defense every time you hear that you have been lied about, misunderstood, or misquoted. If you are innocent, God will see that you are proved so in due time.

◆ Pray through to a forgiving spirit on your part, and prove your forgiving spirit by a forgiving tongue.

◆ Admit to yourself and to God that at least a part of the blame for the disagreement may be yours.

◆ Seek to see the other person's viewpoint of the issue. Place yourself in his or her surroundings and background.

◆ Honestly look for some justifiable motive on the part of your opposer for his or her action.

◆ Make apologies even when there may be doubt that you owe them. This is going the second mile.

◆ Be slow to demand apologies and repayment from your opposer, even when you are sure they are due.

◆ Take the scriptural path toward the solution of the difference as outlined in Matt. 5:23-24.

◆ Try to make friends of your opposition. Go about this very slowly, sincerely, and prayerfully. God and time are your allies.

◆ Shut the door on the past. Do your best to fix things up, and then quit talking about it. Don't let others talk to you about it. Quit thinking about it. Commit to God, and take your hands off.

Prayer: *O Christ, when I differ from somebody, help me to show a noncritical spirit.*

The Enabling Eleventh Commandment

Scripture: "'Love the Lord your God with all your heart . . . soul . . . strength and . . . mind'; and, 'Love your neighbor as yourself.'"
(Luke 10:27, NIV)

The 11th commandment is the word of Jesus to love God sincerely. The Ten Commandments tell us what to do (or not to do), while the 11th commandment states the enabling power: love. Here is grace at its greatest and humanity at their highest. Pure, divine love brings heaven to hearth and a holy God to human hearts.

The nature of this love is: (1) emotional—"with all your heart"; (2) sincere—"with all your soul"; (3) energetic—"with all your strength"; (4) intelligent—"with all your mind"; and (5) unselfish—"your neighbor as yourself" (Luke 10:27, NIV).

This love is expressed in a fathomless consecration. We give ourselves completely to God—heart, soul, strength, and mind. We hold nothing back. We take our hands off what already belongs to God. There are no secret sins; no inner reservations. We belong to God from the top of our heads to the bottom of our feet. And we express this love in more than a passive good will to our neighbors; it is an active, loving, joyful, witnessing, compelling force that points Godward.

This love bears fruit in a cheerful obedience, in an affection for God's people, in a right relationship with everyone, and in a moving compassion for the unsaved everywhere. It detaches one's affection from worldly things and strengthens one's affections for spiritual things.

The proof of this love is found in the purity of our love toward God and the passion and action of our love toward people. Those who have it not only keep the other commandments but also seek to please God always and win people everywhere.

Prayer: *Father, enable me to love You and others sincerely, completely, and unselfishly!*

The Golden Rule Beyond Grade School

Scripture: "Do nothing out of selfish ambition
or vain conceit."

(Phil. 2:3, NIV)

The Golden Rule we learned in childhood has expanding dimensions for the maturing Christian.

◆ *Observe the law of spiritual reciprocity.* Treat others as you would be treated. Give as you wish to be given to.

◆ *Observe the law of divine reciprocity.* Judge others as you wish to be judged by God. Be slow to question the motives of others; only God knows their hearts. He forbids us to judge for our own good and for the good of others.

◆ *Eliminate the ulterior.* Pure motives are necessary for pure acts. Do what you do for others in a childlike sincerity without scheming to receive.

◆ *Do favors without expecting favors in return.* Love does not give selfishly or do good deeds only to receive good deeds in return.

◆ *Be slow to expose the faults of others.* When tempted to repeat gossip, ask yourself: Is it true? Is it necessary that I repeat it? Am I repeating it in kindness? Be quick to expose your own sins to God and seek forgiveness. Exposing the sins of others is God's business alone.

◆ *Avoid tricks, schemes, and deals* that will put you under obligation to other people or that will put other people under obligation to you. Keep your soul, your thoughts, and your actions free.

◆ *Always place the best interpretation upon the actions of other people.* Be eager to believe the best of every person in every circumstance. Should a brother stumble, it is better to be caught in the act of lifting him up than kicking him further down.

Prayer: *Lord, give me not only good sense in dealing with others but also a humble spirit that seeks no personal advantage.*

Some Debts I Gladly Pay

Scripture: "Therefore . . . we have an obligation."
(Rom. 8:12, NIV)

◆ *My testimony.* "Let the redeemed of the Lord say so." Look what God has done for me! How can I keep silent about His goodness? I cannot plead timidity, for I speak up about other good things. I will therefore tell all of His goodness, His grace, His mercy to me. I owe that to God.

◆ *My faithful attendance in worship.* I owe this because it is His house and I am His child. He has commanded: "Forsake not the assembling of yourselves together." I will keep that commandment, without looking for an excuse to miss. I love my church, and I prove my love by my faithfulness.

◆ *My service to Him.* His commission is: "Go ye into all the world, and preach the gospel to every creature" (Mark 16:15). It is not simply the responsibility of my pastor nor of missionaries in another hemisphere; it is also my work here in my community. I owe God the work of teaching, visiting, calling, praying, and witnessing. When there is physical work or repairs to be done at the church, I owe God my service to His house. If I spend all my working hours for myself and my own income, I have missed the debt I owe God.

◆ *My generosity.* My tithes and offerings are freely given to God. He has been so generous to me. How can I be any less in response to Him? It is not only a debt I owe but a gift of thanksgiving.

I owe God. I am responsible. I am in debt. And gladly I pay!

Prayer: *Lord, keep me always conscious of the debt I owe You.*

The Buck Stops Here

Scripture: "Each of us then will have to answer
for himself to God."

(Rom. 14:12, MOFFATT)

My first responsibility is to God. On that final day I must stand
before Him, without excuses, to be judged.

◆ *I am responsible to God for my thoughts.* Do I allow, entertain,
and enjoy ungodly thoughts? Do I fail to dispel them immediately?

◆ *I am responsible to God for my attitudes.* Am I sour? Critical? Negative? Domineering? Carnal? Am I hurt when I cannot have my own way?

◆ *I am responsible to God for my words.* Does slang often pass
from my lips? Do I fuss? Nag? Say cutting things? Am I careless
with my conversation?

◆ *I am responsible to God for my time.* Do I waste time on the
job, thereby stealing money from my employer? Do I spend too
much time with the TV, the telephone, the newspaper? Do I focus on
the important things in life?

◆ *I am responsible to God for my money.* Am I giving generously
to His kingdom? Am I spending the remainder of my money wisely?

◆ *I am responsible to God for my talents.* Am I willing to teach a
class? Repair the church? Work in the nursery?

◆ *I am responsible to God for my friends and coworkers.* Have I told
them of Christ's love? Have I shared the miraculous change in my life?

◆ *I am responsible to God for my family.* Do I share this spiritual responsibility with my spouse? Do I make family devotions a priority? Do I make a conscious effort to lead my children to Christ?

◆ *I am responsible to God for my church.* Do I pray for my pastor? Do I share the burden equally with him?

◆ *I am responsible to God for my opportunities.* Do I remember
that every day I face people who need God? Do I take each opportunity given to me to share Christ?

Prayer: *Lord, burden me with a desire to accept personal responsibility
for my relationship with You and all that it involves!*

Twenty-two Ways to Lie

Scripture: "You must not tell lies."   (Deut. 5:20, TLB)

◆ Twisting words: making a person say something he did not say.
◆ Twisting truth: clever wording to make a lie out of the truth.
◆ Shading the truth: perverting of the facts.
◆ Misstatement of facts: just a plain, unvarnished lie.
◆ Jumping to conclusions: assuming you know when you do not know.
◆ Crafty questions: creating doubt and unwarranted suspicion.
◆ Bodily movements: a wink, a nod, a smile conveying deception.
◆ Slandering: uttering false charges that damage reputation.
◆ Gossiping: indulging in sensational, negative, and harmful chatter.
◆ Judging: arriving at a verdict of guilty without all the facts.
◆ Exaggerating: enlarging a thing beyond the bounds of truth.
◆ Presuming: backing up accusations by probability instead of facts.
◆ Accusations: condemning a person on purely circumstantial evidence.
◆ Insinuations: making statements that leave untruthful impressions.
◆ Inference: reasoning without evidence.
◆ Innuendo: reflecting on one's character or reputation.
◆ Surmise: placing guilt when the evidence is scanty or slight.
◆ Suspicion: casting a cloud of mistrust without sufficient truth.
◆ Silence: withholding information which would clear the "guilty" one.
◆ Flattery: praising insincerely and excessively from motives of self-interest.
◆ Quotations: making another person do your lying for you.
◆ White lies: just plain black lies some hypocrite has tried to whitewash.

Prayer: *God, help me to tell just the truth, the whole truth, and nothing but the truth in such a way and with such timing as to be honest.*

Grand Theft

Scripture: "You must not steal."
(Deut. 5:19, TLB)

◆ *I will not steal from God by taking His day and making it my own.* It is not my day. God gives me six days for myself, so I will keep His day holy in His name.

◆ *I will not steal from God the time He has entrusted to me.* Every minute I have on this earth is a gift from Him, and I am responsible for its use. Therefore, I will not waste time while so many are desperately lost.

◆ *I will not steal from God by desecrating the temple of my body.* Since He lives in me and owns my body, I will take care to keep myself pure. I will not harm my body with destructive habits. I will not bring on disease by overeating and neglect of rest.

◆ *I will not steal from God by neglecting the opportunities He has given me for doing good.* I will not fail to witness, serve, and study His Word.

◆ *I will not steal from my employer by failing to give a full day's work for a full day's pay.* Whether I have agreed to work for $5 per hour or $20 per hour, I will give my diligent best.

◆ *I will not steal from myself by refusing to employ my talents for Christ and the church.* I will be on time. I will participate by singing, standing, kneeling, giving, reading, working, calling, and teaching as opportunity affords.

I will not rob God, nor people, nor myself. Instead of taking, I will give to others in the same way He has so generously given to me.

Prayer: *Broaden my concept of needful ownership, Lord, so that I do not become careless about the things I desire.*

A Pack of Thieves

Scripture: "You shall not steal."
(Exod. 20:15, NIV)

◆ The violent thief takes another's money, possessions, or life.

◆ The cunning thief makes counterfeit money or passes hot checks.

◆ The amateur thief shoplifts articles from the department store, the office, or the workplace.

◆ The extortion thief demands unjust rent or interest rates.

◆ The forgetful thief "forgets" to return borrowed books or money.

◆ The classroom thief cheats on tests or reports by stealing someone else's answers.

◆ The honorable thief finds legal loopholes.

◆ The dishonorable thief steals from the poor, the helpless, the child, the widow, or even the church.

◆ The lazy thief takes pay for work he does not do.

◆ The charity thief draws welfare when he could be working.

◆ The time thief is always late to work, appointments, and church.

◆ The reputation thief steals the good name of others.

◆ The self thief robs himself of health, happiness, and salvation.

◆ The neglectful thief keeps intending to pay his pledges, his bills, and his debts but never does.

◆ The word thief claims credit for what other people have written or said.

◆ The God thief withholds his tithe and offerings.

◆ The church thief accepts the position but not the responsibility.

◆ The soul thief causes the weaker Christian to doubt, to stumble, or to give up.

Prayer: *O Lord, remove any desire within me that makes me put any person or possession before You.*

The Cancer of Coveting

Scripture: "You shall not covet."
(Deut. 5:21, NASB)

The first nine commandments deal largely with our outward acts and relationships, while the tenth deals with our inner motives and desires. In this respect it is a bridge from the laws of "dos and don'ts" to the law of grace and inner cleansing.

Covetousness speaks of an unlawful desire, an unholy ambition, an unexpressed selfishness, a dangerous wish, a damning yearning. From these evil roots grow the noxious weeds of inner warfare, the cutting blade of the carnal spirit, the sharp thorn of sinful indulgence.

The symptoms of covetousness are many. There is a thirst for the forbidden, a spirit of complaining and discontent, a carnal greed, a thankless disposition. There is the jealous fear of being replaced by a rival. There is the fleshly self-esteem of pride. There is the bitterness of envy, lust, greed, and self. There is the idea that everyone else is wrong. There is the grudging of the enemy's good and the rejoicing in the enemy's failure. Theirs is the proud flesh of the spirit revealed in a hurt attitude. The eye is constantly on position, promotion, and possessions.

The cure for covetousness is not found in denying desires. The sinful nature must be cleansed. The Holy Spirit must flood the uttermost part of the inner being. God must spiritualize the whole. He must control the heart. Then the root of covetousness is replaced by peace.

Prayer: *God, You have commanded me to keep my hands off many things. Teach me the folly of wanting the wrong things.*

Growing and Maturing

Down Deep/Up High

Scripture: "Just as you received Christ . . . ,
continue to live in him."   (Col. 2:6, NIV)

In his classic book *Perfect Love*, Dr. J. A. Wood notes these differences between purity and maturity:

◆ Purity is moral cleanness; maturity is moral stature and strength.

◆ Purity is our privilege and duty now; maturity is a question of time.

◆ Purity is instantaneous; maturity is gradual.

◆ No Christian is cleansed into maturity, nor do any grow into purity.

◆ Purity suggests condition, while maturity suggests degrees of advancement.

◆ Purity is always a prerequisite to heaven; maturity never is.

We will not all attain the same level of maturity. However, we all must advance steadily toward maturity after our new birth in Christ. In Col. 2:6-7, Paul pictures growth in a graphic way—down deep and up high.

◆ *Rooted.* After some nearby trees had been harvested, a few tall trees were left to stand alone. Despite their height, they were subsequently toppled by an insignificant storm. Why? Previously surrounded by other trees, they had never been exposed to the stress of storms and consequently had not put down deep roots. The lonely, exposed oak on the crest of the hill is rooted of necessity. This rooting process is imperative for Christians, too, if they are to grow to maturity.

◆ *Built up.* The superstructure of a tree must also be strong. This sometimes involves pruning, a painful but beautifying process. Sometimes the storms twist the branches so that they grow in grotesque beauty and strength. The growing down by the roots and the growing up by the branches is the process that establishes the Christian in the faith.

◆ *Fruitful.* Perhaps this is the ultimate test of maturity. It is not enough to stand amid the storm. There must also be fruit-bearing reproduction. Are you a productive Christian?

Prayer: *Lord, teach me that to continue in You I must grow up in You.*

When Recess Is Over

Scripture: "Then we will no longer be infants . . .
Instead . . . we will . . . grow up."
(Eph. 4:14-15, NIV)

People are not necessarily mature because they have grown older. Nor are Christians mature because they are saved and Spirit-filled. While purity is instantaneous, maturity is gradual. It is the result of growth, study, improvement, and achievement. In Eph. 4 Paul gives us some obvious markings of Christian maturity.

◆ *Acceptance of instruction* (v. 11). The immature "know it all," but the mature are teachable and humble. They constantly seek to learn, develop, and improve.

◆ *Usefulness in service* (v. 12). A colt first runs alongside its mother, who is harnessed to the plow. But later the colt is mature enough to be trained for service also. Childhood is play time. Youth is preparation time. Maturity is serving time. We cannot spend all our lives playing and preparing. There is spiritual work to do!

◆ *Stability of purpose* (v. 14). Mature Christians are not distracted by minor disruptions. They are living on purpose. They are not lured by attractive alternatives to God's plan.

◆ *Ability to be governed by principle instead of passion* (v. 15). Humanity flares into temper. The emotions of mature Christians are Spirit-controlled.

◆ *Cooperation in activity* (v. 16). Children are not always cooperative. They would sometimes rather sulk, pout, argue, cry, and even quit than cooperate. Such actions among adults indicate a lack of spiritual maturity.

◆ *Settled faith* (v. 21). Mature Christians have found solid ground in the Lord as ultimate Authority. For them there can be no question mark where God has put a period.

Prayer: *God, save me from perpetual spiritual infancy.
Make me hunger for growth.*

Growing Tall in the Son

Scripture: "But if we walk in the light . . . the blood of
Jesus . . . purifies us from all sin."

(1 John 1:7, NIV)

When I was a boy rounding up cattle, we had one very promi-
nent landmark on the farm—a bent and gnarled mesquite tree. No
one knew what caused the tree to twist. Maybe a stampede had tram-
pled it when it was young or perhaps lightning struck it. We also had
a crooked calf in the herd. Soon after birth he contracted an infection
that left him so unsightly that my brother named him "Lazarus." Nature has its strange imperfections.

So does the human race. Almost any pastor could write a book
on *Some Twisted Souls I Have Known*. Some of them live on the
streets or have been institutionalized. They stand at the intersec-
tions begging. Others blend into the culture more subtly. Their lust
for immortality, their professional ambition, their passion for pleasure, and their financial greed thrive in a corrupt society. Whether
accepted or rejected by society, everyone is born with the twist of sin
in his heart.

And this is precisely where the message of holiness shines in
sharpest perspective. The work of the Holy Spirit removes the natural inclination or the "bent to sinning" in the human heart and
cleanses away all the corruption of the carnal nature. This deliverance is necessary if we are to grow symmetrically.

All about us are trophies of grace, lofty examples of once-twist-
ed lives now made straight by the power of the Holy Spirit. The Holy
Spirit can provide all you need for growth in Him.

Prayer: *Lord, help me to obey Your will and to be cleansed
from my desire to run my own life.*

Run for the Gold

Scripture: "Throw off every impediment and the entanglement of sin."   (Heb. 12:1, GOODSPEED)

Heb. 12 depicts the main qualities of successfully running toward a diving goal:

◆ *Prepare for the race.* "Lay aside every weight" (v. 1). Get rid of any excess. Set your priorities, and stick to them.

◆ *Get victory over the one sin in your life.* Usually there is *one* that troubles you most. Is it selfishness? Pride? Greed? Lust? Money? Stubbornness? Deceit? Worry? Fear? Love of pleasure? Unholy ambition? Identify the "sin which doth so easily beset" you (v. 1), "which clings so closely" to you (RSV), "the sin which dogs [your] feet" (PHILLIPS), "every sin to which [you] cling" (NEB). Come to grips with the thing that defeats you so often.

◆ *Cultivate patience.* "Run with patience the race that is set before" you (v. 1). Run your own race, not someone else's. Be patient in your own assignments and responsibilities.

◆ *Keep your eyes on Jesus.* "Looking unto Jesus" (v. 2). Don't pay too much attention to criticism or compliments. He is the One you must please.

◆ *Don't give up.* Avoid mental and spiritual fatigue. "Lest ye be weary and faint in your minds" (v. 3). Guard against discouragement.

◆ *Be cheerful in discipline.* "Endure chastening" (v. 7). As a parent corrects a child whom he or she loves, so Christ disciplines us. Discipline is for your own good. After it is all over, you will see it was best.

◆ *Discipline yourself too.* "Tighten your loosening grip and steady your trembling knees. Keep your feet on a steady path, so that the limping foot does not collapse but recovers strength" (vv. 12-13, PHILLIPS).

◆ *Don't be a troublemaker.* "Follow peace with all men" (v. 14). Be a peacemaker.

◆ *Pursue holiness.* It is the only way you can get to heaven (v. 14). It is the only way you can be victorious here (v. 15).

Prayer: *Father, deepen my faith and my walk with You.*
Teach me the ways of personal maturity.

By the Bushel

Scripture: "By their fruit you will recognize them."
(Matt. 7:20, NIV)

Scientific law teaches four important truths that Jesus used in the Scripture to tell His disciples about spiritual maturity.

◆ *Bearing fruit is the normal process of all life.* If life is healthy, fruit may be expected. The farmer depends on this as he plants the seed. God also depends on this factor in the lives of His disciples. It is the normal process of the healthy Christian to reproduce other Christians. Where there is lack of spiritual reproduction, there is an unhealthy condition in the heart.

◆ *Bearing fruit means reproducing in kind.* Good seed will produce good fruit, and inferior seed will produce inferior fruit. This is true in the church also. Vital, courageous, victorious Christians will reproduce in kind. And careless, prayerless, joyless "saints" will also reproduce in kind.

◆ *Bearing fruit means multiplying in number.* The farmer may plant 5 bushels of seed to the acre, but he expects to harvest 50 bushels of seed from the same acre. He depends on the increase to stay in business. Seventeen men first dedicated themselves to the principles of Communism. Forty-five years later almost 1 billion people were dominated by this atheistic system. As they bore fruit, they multiplied in number. Is this true within your spiritual life? What about your church? Is it larger now than it was five years ago? Will people join you in heaven for eternity because of your influence?

◆ *Bearing fruit is imperative to survival.* Suppose just one generation of cattle should fail to reproduce. The cow would become extinct; there would be no more beef, milk, butter, cheese, or leather. If Christians should stop bearing fruit for one short generation, Christianity would become extinct! Are you bearing fruit for God's kingdom?

Prayer: *Father, help me to be good and faithful so my fruit will be good and faithful.*

Halfway or Summit?

Scripture: "Perseverance must finish its work so that you may be mature and complete, not lacking anything."

(James 1:4, NIV)

Our first trip up Pikes Peak many years ago was marred by several events that caused delays and misgivings. When at last we arrived at the Halfway House, we stopped for rest and to let the car cool. When it was time to move up to the top, certain fearful members of the family balked. They had had enough of steep inclines with no guardrails. And, as they put it, they could see well enough from Halfway House. The scenery was beautiful here, why go all the way up? They even discouraged us from moving upward. So while the rest of us enjoyed the limitless vistas of the summit, they spent their time feeding the chipmunks and dreading the downward trail.

We've all seen it happen in the spiritual realm too. Here and there are Christians who stop at a halfway house in a spiritual sense. They follow Jesus on Sunday morning but live indifferently during the week. They get a taste of glory but still feed on the husks of defeat. They say they love God, but they stop short of serving Him. These fringe people know nothing of the summit of spiritual living.

But, thank God, there are many who go all the way to the peak of spiritual surrender and to the summit of success in the things of God. They have resolutely refused to settle for less than God's best. They are dependable in service to the Body of Christ. They give generously to His kingdom and witness to the lost. Their lives prove they have forsaken all for Him. Thank God for summit Christians.

Prayer: *God, give me enough hunger for fellowship with You that I will climb to the highest point You would take me.*

A Divine Wardrobe

Scripture: "As God's chosen people, . . . clothe
yourselves with compassion, kindness,
humility, gentleness and patience."
(Col. 3:12, NIV)

One of the most humorous books I have seen is titled *The Fine Art of Hypochondria or How Are You?* by Goodman Ace. The title itself is enough to remind us of those idiosyncrasies that we all bear. Some of these are hypochondria, claustrophobia, melancholia, hyperphrasia (talking too much), moodiness, and morbidity. Some are the result of physical conditions; others are related to spiritual needs. Some may be overcome by self-discipline. Still others may simply be personality quirks that are the common lot of all people.

But these idiosyncrasies are not to be confused with the character traits that have a moral and spiritual connotation, as discussed by Paul in Col. 3:12-17. The great apostle considers true holiness as he outlines 10 traits of Christian character that are to be seen in God's people everywhere and at all times.

◆ *Compassion:* sympathetic awareness of distress in other people, plus a desire to alleviate it.

◆ *Kindness:* pleasantness, friendliness, agreeableness; the absence of the cutting tongue, the demanding word, the sarcastic remark.

◆ *Humility:* a spirit of deference or submission; the opposite of arrogance, pride, vanity, self-assertiveness, and conceit.

◆ *Gentleness:* mildness in speech and action, moderate in conduct; the spirit of one who is meek, amiable, peaceable.

◆ *Patience:* long-suffering, bearing of trials without complaint; steadfastness despite opposition or difficulty; willingness to bear.

◆ *Forbearance:* leniency; endurance; doing without; refraining from; abstaining from; controlling oneself when provoked.

◆ *Forgiveness:* ceasing to feel resentment against an offender; pardon; excusing; granting relief from payment of a debt owed.

◆ *Love:* an unselfish concern that freely accepts another in loyalty and seeks his or her good; affectionate concern for others; devotion to God.

◆ *Joy:* an experience of great pleasure or delight; gladness, rejoicing, enjoyment; an emotion evoked by well-being.

◆ *Gratitude:* thankfulness; a state of being grateful; expressing appreciation for benefits received; acknowledgment of favors bestowed.

May we assimilate these ingredients of holy relationships until the child's prayer will be answered in us: "Lord, make all the bad people good, and all the good people nice. Amen."

Prayer: *God, clothe me with character that pleases You,*
and let me resemble Jesus.

Almighty God vs. Almighty Dollar

Scripture: "For where your treasure is, there will
your heart be also."

(Matt. 6:21, NASB)

There are two basic attitudes toward possessions: the selfish
and the spiritual. The selfish attitude says: Things are more important than God; I'll let go of God and get a good grip on things. It is
the attitude of the rich fool, of the robber along the Jericho road, of
the rich young ruler, of Ananias and Sapphira. It is the trademark of
our selfish times, the hallmark of our hollow pleasures, the yardstick of our sensual indulgences. We have demonstrated a more vibrant faith in the almighty dollar than the almighty God. We have
measured success by our salaries and the possessions they buy.

But the spiritual attitude toward possessions says: God is more
important than things; I'll let go of things and get a good grip on
God. It is the attitude of the good Samaritan caring for the half-dead
victim, of the apostle Paul going back to Lystra where they once
stoned him, of Jesus Christ hanging on a shameful cross, of the Early
Church selling their possessions to spread their newfound faith. It is
the trademark of a fathomless consecration, the hallmark of a holy
life, the yardstick of a scriptural spirituality.

It has never been the business of the Church to raise enough
money to keep ourselves in comfort. The business of the Church is
the spreading of the gospel with such compassion that all will come
to the foot of the Cross. In spreading the Good News, the Church will
gladly make sacrifices that are worthy of the agony of Calvary.

Prayer: *Our Father, let nothing become as important to me as You!
You are my highest treasure!*

Wisdom Beyond Wealth

Scripture: "O the depth of the riches and wisdom and knowledge of God! How unsearchable are his judgments." (Rom. 11:33, RSV)

Wisdom that comes from God has beautiful characteristics.

◆ *It is pure.* There is no double-talk in it, no hidden lie. Its aim is to make a correct judgment. There is no moral defilement in the motive.

◆ *It is peaceable.* Its purpose is reconciliation and unity, never agitation or rupture. God is peace; His people are to live in peace.

◆ *It is gentle.* It is never rude, never overbearing, never harsh, never cruel. It is not authoritative or dogmatic. It is firm but kind. It is sure but meek. It is certain without being obnoxious.

◆ *It is easy to be entreated.* It is willing to listen to the other side with sympathy. It is never impatient when contradicted. If discovered to be off the track, wisdom admits it and pulls back. When misunderstandings arise, wisdom peacefully searches for solutions.

◆ *It is full of mercy.* It is humble in victory, never resentful in defeat. It shows kindness to all opposition. It avoids the "I told you so" attitude. It always shows abundant forgiveness.

◆ *It is full of good faith.* It shows kindness to those who are in trouble. It seeks to lift the fallen and to heal the broken.

◆ *It is without partiality.* It plays no favorites. It brushes away the surface and looks for the real facts. It is not impressed with favors. It is not swayed by glamour or wealth. It is interested in fairness.

◆ *It is without hypocrisy.* It allows no tricks, no fraud, no deceit. All pretense, all insincerity, all covered motives are eliminated. "Love . . . without dissimulation" is its motto, and holiness of heart and life is its reward.

Prayer: *God, impart to me enough of Your Spirit that I will have and practice heavenly wisdom.*

The Right Stuff

Scripture: "Listen, my son, and be wise, and keep your heart on the right path."   (Prov. 23:19, NIV)

Proverbs outlines for us several qualities that every growing Christian will have:

◆ *Unreserved commitment* (3:5). Here is the beginning point. Nothing is to be held back. Even our own wisdom and understanding are to be yielded to God.

◆ *Divine guidance* (3:6). The only person God can guide is the one who sincerely seeks for guidance—the one who allows God into all the paths he or she takes.

◆ *Genuine humility* (3:7). The person who is wise in his or her own eyes is really stupid and foolish. We should acknowledge our lack of wisdom and our inabilities.

◆ *Holy separation* (3:7). The separated life has always been the hallmark of holy living. This separation is based on a scriptural "fear of the Lord."

◆ *Developing maturity* (3:8). Few things are more attractive than a sincere desire to grow in the Lord. This is a maturing process that must continue all our lives.

◆ *Wise understanding* (3:13-14). This is not the same as amassing vast knowledge, as valuable as that may be. Understanding includes comprehension and insight.

◆ *Disciplined speech* (15:1-4). If the heart is holy, the tongue is disciplined—even occasionally bitten.

◆ *Controlled affections* (23:19). The heart, like the tongue, must be kept. Affections must never be allowed to run wild. They are always guarded and curbed in harmony with the Word of God and the will of God.

◆ *Hard work* (23:21). Laziness is incompatible with holiness. The indolent, the idle, the slothful, and the sluggish need not only cleansing but also self-discipline. Productive Christians are diligent about the Master's business.

Prayer: *Lord, help me to see the connection between wisdom and correct spiritual direction.*

When God Calls

Scripture: "In all things God works for the good of those who love him, who have been called according to his purpose." (Rom. 8:28, NIV)

There are at least four facets to God's callings:

◆ The *everyone* call: the universal call to all to be saved. God has given us the "whosoever" gospel.

◆ The *all-serve* call: the appeal of the gospel to every Christian to get busy in God's harvest.

◆ The *full-time* call: the appeal to some to lay aside secular employment and work full time for God as pastors, missionaries, and Christian workers. Those who receive this call are especially chosen of God.

◆ The *pinpoint* call: the awareness that there is a particular place in God's kingdom where one must work, such as a certain location or job.

None can escape the first call; everyone is called to repent and obey. No Christian can escape the second call; every Christian is called to serve. God is calling ordinary people into full-time service, and He is calling all other Christians to support them. Those who fail in either group are failing in their obedience to Him. Those who respond in either group are blessed with thrilling rewards. God frequently pinpoints the place of service for His full-time workers. How wonderful to be at that point on the map, regardless of hemisphere, date line, or equator, regardless of rural or urban assignment.

There seems to be a fairly uniform pattern when God calls. First comes the *awareness* that God has a special task. Then comes the *urgency*, the priority of the appeal from above. And always there is some *introspection* and heart-searching. This inevitably results in a sense of personal *unworthiness* for the task. But then comes the divine *promise*, the assurance of His presence all the way. This calls for immediate response in *obedience* to the will of God. And that means *hard work*, which is most rewarding because it produces results by God's help. May each of us be faithful to His call.

Prayer: *Father, You have called me twice: first by love to follow You and second by need to serve others.*

Keeping in Touch

Scripture: "Break up your unplowed ground; for it is time to seek the LORD."

(Hos. 10:12, NIV)

God's prophets speak His word to their generation. They may be ministers or laymen. But they have these uncommon characteristics in common:

◆ *God's true prophets are in touch with God.* They are on speaking terms with divinity. They speak often and listen always. They hold Him in the highest, sacred reverence. They commune with Him at all times and live holy lives.

◆ *God's true prophets are in touch with God's Word.* They read it devotionally each day. They feast upon it as food for their souls.

◆ *God's true prophets are in touch with others.* They are not aloof or inaccessible. They are among people, sharing their burdens, aware of their needs, encouraging them to walk the high road.

◆ *God's true prophets are in step with the times.* They read, study, learn, and prepare. They keep themselves informed. They know how to interpret, to evaluate, and to perceive. They respect the past, but they are aware of the present.

◆ *God's true prophets are alert to significant trends* in politics, in religion, in education, and in society. They see the significance of today's headlines.

◆ *God's true prophets have an insight into the future.* While they are not always foretelling events, they are always alert to the consequences of today's events. They have an anointed common sense.

◆ *God's true prophets courageously rebuke sin, evil, and injustice.* Sometimes this rebuking is costly to them because it offends their contemporaries. But they are marching to the beat of another Drummer.

Do you have the courage to speak God's message to your generation?

Prayer: *Dear Lord, strengthen my voice so that I will speak the truth to those around me.*

How Do I Know If I'm "Spiritual"?

Scripture: "Let your bearing towards one another arise out of your life in Christ Jesus."

(Phil. 2:5, NEB)

I knew a woman who knew the Bible well, but she kept busy with gossip until people dreaded to see her coming. Was she spiritual? I knew a man who gave generously to the church, but he constantly criticized the way the budget was spent. Was he spiritual? I knew a man who seemed to get blessed each time he prayed, but he failed to pay his debts. Was he spiritual?

What is spirituality?

It is not simply one virtue, like truthfulness.

It is not merely one Christian activity, like witnessing.

It is not a select quality of personality, like emotion.

It is not simply a negative attitude toward worldliness.

It is not just a positive attitude or being faithful.

It is not simply a good habit, like daily prayer.

It is not merely a sacrificial spirit in giving.

It is not evidenced by reading the Bible through systematically.

It is more than testifying with emotion.

Spirituality is the sum total of all these things and more. If there is any one term that describes a spiritual person it is *Christlikeness*. Spirituality is Christlikeness in relationships and attitudes all up and down the scale of life—a Christlikeness toward others, toward self, toward things, toward God.

Kneel at His feet to receive spirituality; sit at His feet to learn spirituality; follow in His steps to prove spirituality.

Prayer: *Lord, save me from the peril of being a phony. Help me desire Christlikeness in my walk with You and others.*

The Pulpit and the Pew

Scripture: "Never be lacking in zeal, but keep your
spiritual fervor, serving the Lord."
(Rom. 12:11, NIV)

E. M. Bounds pinpointed our need for strong leadership in troubled times when years ago he said: "The church is looking for better methods; God is looking for better [people]. What the church needs today is not more machinery or better, not new organizations or more novel methods, but [people] whom the Holy Ghost can use . . . mighty in prayer."

Strong leadership is needed today among both the clergy and the laity.

We need men and women in the pulpit:

◆ Who will assume responsibility for an aggressive leadership.

◆ Who know where they are going and how to get there.

◆ Who know the direction the people ought to be going and who know how to get the people going in that direction.

◆ Who believe the gospel is worth promoting and who get busy at it.

◆ Who believe that revivals can be had for a price and who are willing to pay that price.

We need men and women in the pew:

◆ Who will face up to life's priorities with courage.

◆ Who will support an ordinary pastor with an extraordinary loyalty.

◆ Who will gladly change their man-made methods to get some God-given results.

◆ Who will produce a pure and holy witness that will have its impact on the community.

John Wesley said: "Give me one hundred men who fear nothing but sin, and desire nothing but God, and I care not a straw whether they be clergymen or laymen; such alone will shake the gates of hell and set up the kingdom of heaven on earth."

Prayer: *O God, fill us with a new urgency to do Your work
and will this day.*

While We Wait

Scripture: "May the Lord direct your hearts into God's love and Christ's perseverance."

(2 Thess. 3:5, NIV)

What does the Word of God admonish us to do as we await Christ's return?

◆ *Don't panic.* "Be not soon shaken in mind, or be troubled" (2 Thess. 2:2). Unlike some who react in fear at His coming, we can have peace and confidence.

◆ *Watch for the signs.* Jesus, Paul, Peter, and others gave many signs of the Second Coming. Know what these are and watch for their fulfillment (vv. 3-4).

◆ *Hold steady* (v. 15). Check what you read against God's Word. Refuse to be swept off your feet by false doctrine. God's Word is a sure foundation, even in the end times.

◆ *Love God* (3:5). The person who keeps his or her affections set on things above is not only ready for the Second Coming, but he is also trying to get others ready.

◆ *Be patient.* Paul speaks of "the patient waiting for Christ" (3:5). "Be not weary in well doing" (v. 13). Don't let your courage fade.

◆ *Live the separated life* (3:6, 14). One of the most important things a person can do while waiting for the Lord's return is "to keep himself unspotted from the world" (James 1:27). This is not monastic living; it is holy living among sinful people.

◆ *Work before you eat.* Pull your own weight. "If any would not work, neither should he eat" (2 Thess. 3:10).

◆ *Self-control* (vv. 11-12). Personal discipline is almost a lost art in some places. Christians should set the pattern as they wait for our Lord's return.

◆ *Witness to the non-Christian.* Paul says we are to "Admonish him as a brother" (v. 15). Is there anything more important than winning the lost in these last days? The time is short. The need is great.

◆ *Be peace-keepers* . . . "peace always by all means" (v. 16). Peace is a matter of the inner heart. Let's keep the peace until the Prince of Peace returns.

Prayer: *God, I want to be found safe in Your love and Christ's perseverance. Help me hold true.*

Sign-Watching

Scripture: "You know very well that the day of the Lord will come like a thief in the night."

(1 Thess. 5:2, NIV)

Though we do not know when Jesus will return, the Scripture is clear about the signs of His coming:

◆ *Diplomatic signs:* "When they shall say, Peace and safety; then sudden destruction cometh upon them" (1 Thess. 5:3).

◆ *Political signs:* "For nation shall rise against nation, and kingdom against kingdom" (Matt. 24:7).

◆ *Commercial signs:* "Ye have heaped treasure together for the last days" (James 5:3).

◆ *Doctrinal signs:* "For the time will come when they will not endure sound doctrine; . . . they shall turn away their ears from the truth, and shall be turned unto fables" (2 Tim. 4:3-4).

◆ *Natural signs:* "There will be famines, and pestilences, and earthquakes, in divers places" (Matt. 24:7).

◆ *Ecclesiastical signs:* "That day shall not come, except there come a falling away first" (2 Thess. 2:3).

◆ *Moral signs:* "Men shall be lovers of their own selves, covetous, boasters, proud, blasphemers, disobedient to parents, unthankful, unholy, without natural affection, trucebreakers, false accusers, incontinent, fierce, despisers of those that are good, traitors, heady, highminded, lovers of pleasures more than lovers of God" (2 Tim. 3:2-4).

◆ *Evangelical signs:* "And this gospel of the kingdom shall be preached in all the world . . . and then shall the end come" (Matt. 24:14).

◆ *Cultic signs:* "And many false prophets shall rise, and deceive many" (Matt. 24:11).

◆ *Spiritual signs:* "Having a form of godliness, but denying the power thereof" (2 Tim. 3:5). "And because iniquity shall abound, the love of many shall wax cold" (Matt. 24:12).

◆ *Scoffer signs:* "Where is the promise of his coming?" (2 Pet. 3:4).

◆ *Persecution signs:* "Then shall they deliver you up to be afflicted, and shall kill you" (Matt. 24:9).

Prayer: *Lord, keep me close to You so that I will be ready to meet You when You come for me.*

Resurrection Call

Scripture: "We will not all sleep, but we will all be changed—in a flash, in the twinkling of an eye."

(1 Cor. 15:51-52, NIV)

In his famous resurrection chapter (1 Cor. 15), Paul discusses three last things that give us glorious hope for eternity.

◆ *"The last Adam"* (v. 45). Christ is the focal Figure of the picture. Paul contrasts Adam with Christ. The first Adam who died is compared with the last Adam, the crucified Christ who lives. He states that "in Adam all die, even so in Christ all shall be made alive" (v. 22). "The first man [Adam] is of the earth . . . : the second man is the Lord from heaven" (v. 47). The first Adam plunged the race into sin; the second provided the remedy for sin. The first brought death to every man; the second brought resurrection to every man.

◆ *"The last enemy"* (v. 26). Death is not only the last enemy but also the ultimate enemy. Death is the completed work of Satan— his capstone. "Sin, when it is finished, bringeth forth death" (James 1:15). This death is not only physical but, worst of all, it is spiritual. That is why God sent the last Adam to deal with the last enemy so that He might defeat the devil at the point of his greatest triumph— death. Thus we understand that if God can destroy death, our ultimate enemy, He can handle every other problem.

◆ *"The last trump"* (v. 52). God's trumpet will ultimately sound the signal for all who are dead in Christ to come forth from their graves wearing their resurrection bodies. In the twinkling of an eye, this last sound of the trumpet will change every living Christian from his or her present mortal body to that immortal and incorruptible state of the glorified (vv. 52-53). At the last trump, the last Adam will order the last enemy to be "swallowed up in victory" (v. 54).

Prayer: *May Your name be praised, O God! You have conquered death. With Christ's resurrection, ours is promised.*

Don't Spare the Thanks

Scripture: "Were not all ten cleansed? Where are the other nine? Was no one found to return and give praise to God except this foreigner?"   (Luke 17:17-18, NIV)

During the battle of Dunkirk an old minister who was serving a church in a small coastal town of England noticed that a young boy came to pray in the church each day at noon. On the fifth day the preacher watched in silence while the boy prayed alone. When he had finished his devotions the minister asked him, "May I help you? Do you have a relative in the battle at Dunkirk?"

The boy lifted his tear-stained face and answered, "I did have a relative at Dunkirk, sir. It was my dad. But he came home last night. I prayed for him for four days. So today I wanted to come back and thank God for bringing him home to us."

This boy was a craftsman in the fine art of being thankful. In addition to asking God for favors, he took time out to thank God who granted the favors. To learn this fine art of thanksgiving, we must consider some basic factors.

◆ We cannot truthfully say that God has ever been unfair to us.

◆ We must honestly admit that God's mercy is unfailing to us.

◆ We do not deserve many of the blessings God gives us.

◆ We often take for granted some of life's choicest blessings.

◆ Giving thanks is both an attitude and an expression of that attitude.

◆ We cannot be truly thankful without showing it.

◆ True gratitude makes us appreciate the giver more than the gift.

◆ Thanks must be expressed or it will die of neglect.

◆ Thankful living purifies and fortifies the inner self.

◆ The truly thankful demonstrate this quality to people and God alike.

Prayer: *Father, remind me to make my praise specific rather than general and often rather than rare.*

The Wisest of All

Scripture: "We saw his star in the east and have come
to worship him."

(Matt. 2:2, NIV)

We learn from the wise men lessons of worship that last all year.

◆ *They had wisdom to follow the guidance of God* (v. 2*b*). They
had willingly been following God's star for perhaps as long as two
years. They allowed God to guide them.

◆ *They had wisdom to admit they did not know all the answers*
(v. 2*a*). Some of us are ashamed to ask questions for fear the questions will betray our ignorance. But without false pride the wise
men asked, "Where is he?"

◆ *They had wisdom to depend upon the written Word of God* (v.
5). God's star did not hold all the answers, so they looked into His
written Word.

◆ *They had wisdom to recognize God in unlikely circumstances*
(v. 8). Go to Bethlehem? Why not Jerusalem, the center of govern-
ment, population, religion, commerce, and industry? Nevertheless,
they trusted God.

◆ *They had wisdom to rejoice that they were in the will of God* (v.
10). Perhaps they were perplexed, but they were happy in God's will.
We all have a right to rejoice when we are in the will of God.

◆ *They had the wisdom to offer more than lip service as they wor-
shiped the King* (v. 11). They brought sacrificial gifts—not because
the Holy Child needed them but because they could not come empty-
handed into the presence of the King.

◆ *They had wisdom to let God upset their plans* (v. 12). They
had followed the gleam of God to this glad hour with good success.
Why not trust His guidance in the journey to come?

Prayer: *Lord, give me the certain trust and strong determination
to worship You as the wise men did.*

Silence Broken

Scripture: "With many other words he warned them;
and he pleaded with them."

(Acts 2:40, NIV)

Side by side they worked eight hours a day, five days a week, for nearly a month. They discussed politics, business, sports, new automobiles, the weather, the boss, their homes, their friends, and the stock market. They became good friends. Then at the end of the month, they bumped into each other at a city-wide Christian rally. Both were amazed. Both were professing Christians and had not discussed it. Both were chagrined that they had professed Christ so silently at work. Both were victims of Satan's fatal half-true philosophy, which says, "The best witness is the silent witness. Sermons are better seen than heard. Christians are lights, and lights do not talk; they just shine."

For the most part, the silent witness is no witness at all. What value would a judge and jury find in a witness who knew the facts but who refused to talk? Whoever took the witness stand and "let his light shine"? Witnesses must tell what they know or they are not witnesses. They must tell it when personal inconvenience is involved, when personal threats impend, when others do not want to hear the truth.

The Holy Spirit's power has a way of removing padlocks of fear from frozen jaws, of urging Christians to take the witness stand and spell out what they know to be true. Peter and John were silent witnesses in Gethsemane, at the trial of Jesus, on bloody Calvary, and even beyond Easter's glory. But Pentecost put within them a courage to witness unafraid and unashamed in the face of chains, whips, and death. They had an experience that would not keep unless it was shared, that meant so much to them that they had to tell others.

Prayer: *Teach me, Lord, never to be an indifferent witness.*

Facing the Risks

Scripture: "The apostles left the Sanhedrin, rejoicing because they had been counted worthy of suffering disgrace for the Name."

(Acts 5:41, NIV)

There are some calculated risks in witnessing that may deter the casual Christian's effort to present Christ to his or her friends.

◆ *The risk of being considered* narrow. We fear that the other person may look upon us as limited in our scope and restricted in our views because we are presenting the God instead of a god. Let us not forget, however, that Jesus himself spoke of the "narrow" as the only way.

◆ *The risk of appearing* prejudiced. We are afraid the non-Christian will accuse us of having closed minds, a preconceived position with sufficient facts. We abhor the idea of an irrational attitude toward others. We reject the thought of being hostile toward individuals or groups outside our circle. Yet the risk is real, because Christians have a natural "bias" in favor of Jesus Christ.

◆ *The risk of seeming to be* dogmatic. In these times when the educated often seem unsure of everything, Christians may be reluctant to insist on a definite, authoritative conclusion. But humanity's mind and heart reach out for certainty and assurance. The Bible says there is no other way.

◆ *The risk of being called* puritanical. We may be afraid that no one will be interested in a religion that demands truth, honesty, and holiness. The sinful reject spiritual, moral, and ethical demands, but Christians cannot compromise.

◆ *The risk of being thought* opinionated. This risk smacks of pride, and holy people shun pride. But we know we are right because the Bible is right; we cannot yield our position for lesser theories.

How can we have courage to witness in the face of such risks? Three things will help us: (1) We must be sure that we are living righteous lives ourselves; (2) We must use all the common sense we can muster when confronting people with the claims of Christ; and (3) We must overflow with love as we tell them of Jesus. When we do these things, God will go before us and prepare the way. We can leave the results with Him.

Prayer: *Father, I am willing to be an unashamed witness, risk or no risk.*

The Deserted Waterpot

Scripture: "A good many believed in Him because of the woman's statement."

(John 4:39, WEYMOUTH)

When the sinful woman of Samaria met Christ at Jacob's Well and received His forgiveness, she left her waterpot and went rejoicing on her way to witness to what had happened to her.

This deserted waterpot tells us that *Jesus majored on soul winning.* He sought out people everywhere: up trees, in boats, among the tombs, beside waters, in the Temple, along the dusty roadside. He preached to the masses, but he forgave individuals.

The deserted waterpot suggests that *Christ satisfies* the God-hungry, the confused, the sin-sick, the frustrated. This woman had run the gamut of earthly pleasure-hunting yet was still empty in her heart and thirsty in her soul. She discovered what every person must honestly admit: There is no satisfaction outside the will of God. Christ satisfies abundantly.

The deserted waterpot also reminds us that *it is a normal thing for spiritual people to witness.* Jesus did not beg her to tell it. She was eager to share. She was not content to sit complacently at the feet of her Lord, enjoying her newfound deliverance, while her friends stumbled on in their darkness and defeat. She had found the joyful way of living victory, and she wanted to share this blessing. If Christians are not witnessing, it is because they are not normal, healthy, and well-fed.

The deserted waterpot also gives us the assurance that Christians live out their witness. This Christ-transformed woman went home to witness where she was best known. The whole town was stirred at her testimony, backed up by her changed life. People will always be affected for good when they see God-inspired changes in our daily lives.

Prayer: *Lord, show me the "waterpots" I could do without and still be an effective witness for You.*

Overcoming Roadblocks
to Faith

Does Jesus Care About Me?

Scripture: "Throw all your anxiety upon him, for he cares for you." (1 Pet. 5:7, GOODSPEED)

Does Jesus care? This is one of the most important questions we can ask about Him—and one of the most often asked too. The disciples asked it when the storm was raging and He was asleep in the floundering boat. As His disciples, we are still asking the same question—not because we don't believe, but because we need reassurance that His care is personally applicable.

The mother asks the question when her child suffers dreadfully and relief does not come. The homeowner asks it when the storm levels her house and all her cherished possessions are swept away. The pastor asks it when his preaching meets resistance. The young Christian asks it when temptation comes in like a flood and Satan seems about to pull him beneath the waves. The victor asks it when an unexplained accident disables him for life.

Does Jesus care? Christians everywhere throughout the centuries have answered with a resounding "Yes! Jesus does care!"

Sometimes He shows that care in ways that we least expect and perhaps do not appreciate at the moment. Paul prayed three times for life's sharp thorn to be taken out of his flesh—but the thorn remained so that Paul might learn that the presence of grace was better than the absence of a thorn. Often God does remove the thorn. But if not, He still cares. And He has a better answer.

Does Jesus care? It is a question that demands action from us too. Jesus spent His entire ministry on earth in compassion for hurting hearts, minds, and bodies. If we are His, this is our ministry too. We are most like Him when we are touching others with His love. Holy living is never complete while shut up in a closet; it reaches its fullest dimensions only through human contact—witnessing, sharing, loving, helping, visiting, encouraging, lifting.

Jesus cares. Am I like Him?

Prayer: *God, we praise You this day for caring for our every anxiety, fear, and concern.*

If Only Temptation Weren't So Tempting!

Scripture: "Blessed is the man who perseveres under trial, because when he has stood the test, he will receive the crown of life."

(James 1:12, NIV)

Five facets of temptation are clearly pointed out in 1 Cor. 10:13.

◆ *Everyone is tempted.* The young and the old—the weak and the strong—the disciplined and the careless—the learned and the unlearned. Every Christian is tempted. Paul said temptation was universal—"common to man."

◆ *God is faithful.* God is dependable and can be trusted. You are not in the struggle alone. God will not desert you. He is personal, present, and caring.

◆ *God limits temptation.* He "will not suffer you to be tempted above that ye are able." God draws the line and tells Satan to stop. He limits the extent to which Satan can saddle you with temptation. This does not mean that all are overcomers. It does mean that all *may* overcome. If not, the blame is not on God, for He limits the temptation. If we yield, the failure is ours, for we have a way to conquer.

◆ *God opens the door of deliverance.* He is always on hand to "make a way to escape." He may not pull you through the door of deliverance, but He unlocks the door, opens it, and beckons you to victorious living.

◆ *God has purpose in temptation:* "that ye may be able to bear it" and be strengthened by it. Victory over temptation produces strength. Spiritual giants are made in the valley of temptation by overcoming.

Prayer: *Lord, remind me that the real reward for faithfulness to You is in the life to come. Help me willingly to accept delayed reward.*

I Thought I Was Exempt

Scripture: "I will not forget you! See, I have engraved you on the palms of my hands."

(Isa. 49:15*c*-16, NIV)

◆ Suffering is universal. Everyone is exposed. Salvation is not an insurance policy against trouble.

◆ God permits suffering. He could have prevented it, but He didn't. Perhaps only God knows why you suffer. Perhaps He is not in a hurry to answer your "Why?" Learn patience in suffering.

◆ Do not blame yourself as you suffer.

◆ Do not indulge in self-pity.

◆ Do not advertise your suffering. God knows and cares.

◆ You may suffer innocently, through no fault of your own. Leave the vindication to God.

◆ The evil who deserve to suffer often seem to live in ease. Do not let this shake your faith, for you do not know all the facts nor all the future.

◆ Forgive those who may cause your undeserved suffering— even if they do not deserve forgiveness.

◆ Let God punish those who deserve to be punished. Let Him be their Judge. If He chooses to be merciful with your enemies, remember that He was also merciful with you.

◆ Avoid resentment in your suffering.

◆ Let God speak to you through your suffering. It's time to listen.

◆ Time is in your favor. Let time help heal your hurt.

◆ Suffering is temporary. You are immortal. God is eternal.

◆ Suffering, like rain, will make roses or mud depending on how it is received.

Prayer: *Thank You, Lord, not only for watching over me but also for never forgetting about me. You are a wonderful God!*

Has God Retired?

Scripture: "For God is not a God of disorder but of peace."
(1 Cor. 14:33, NIV)

Has God retired? Has He assumed an inactive relationship so far as world affairs are concerned? Has He become the cosmic Absentee from global distress? Is He no longer interested in what happens to the masses?

What is God like? Is He the kind of person who winds up mechanical humanity much like a boy winds up a toy to let it walk in circles or wander to the edge of the table and smash itself to pieces on the floor below? Is God powerless to curb the direction of humanity's freedom?

Where does God's freedom end and man's begin? Why did God let His enemies slaughter His people? Why does God let our enemies devise weapons that may level us to dust? If God can stop it, then why doesn't He? Is He lacking in love? Does Jesus care? Does He allow humanity to abound in evil because He is weak and can do nothing about it?

These are questions that trouble some good people. They find it possible to believe in a personal God but difficult to believe that God is doing much about the ills of the world in general. They can find adequate faith for themselves but little faith for the nations.

To accomplish His righteous purpose in history, God works in at least two ways: by His moral laws, which bless us or punish us according to our response, and by supernatural intervention either direct or indirect. God alone chooses how He will intervene. His pattern of world events unfolds with infinite patience—so gradually that we hardly notice. We need to look backward from the inspiration point of panoramic faith. We gain confidence when we see His mighty acts throughout history. We gain hope for the future. Are we fully cooperative with the God who guides destinies? We can be an integral part of His plan of order for the entire world.

Prayer: *We praise You, Father, for Your orderliness. It prompts us to order our lives after You.*

Victim Mentality

Scripture: "You can hold me personally responsible."
(Gen. 43:9, NIV)

Making excuses is the oldest of all arts in humanity's attempt to exonerate itself. In the victim mentality of our society, we all sometimes play this game.

◆ *My spouse made me do it.* This was Adam's excuse to God and still one of the favorites of husbands and wives alike.

◆ *The devil made me do it.* This was Eve's excuse, but it is as modern as those who joke about it.

◆ *I can't help it; God made me like I am.* When we lay all our faults on God's creative act, we proclaim ourselves innocent and God guilty.

◆ *My parents are to blame.* They had too many rules . . . They forced me to go to church . . . They were too strict . . . These are the excuses of an entire generation.

◆ *It's the church's fault.* Hypocrites, fire-and-brimstone preaching, rules and regulations . . . Too many people see the church as an easy target to blame.

◆ *It's my nerves.* Stress is common to all of us, but how we handle it is up to us.

Whatever our situation today, we are responsible for our own actions and our own attitudes. When we stand before God for judgment, we must give an account only for ourselves.

Prayer: *Dear Lord, I'm responsible for my own actions and attitudes. Help me to accept responsibility and not blame others.*

When I Don't Know Why

Scripture: "Consider it pure joy . . . whenever you face trials . . . because you know that the testing of your faith develops perseverance."

(James 1:2-3, NIV)

Why do we suffer? We may bring suffering on ourselves. When we drive carelessly, we may have a wreck; when we eat too much, we may get sick. We may bring suffering on ourselves by our own willfulness and sin. Physical habits often have long-term consequences.

◆ *Our enemies may make us suffer.* Just as prisoners of war have been tortured by their captors, vicious lies have been told for the sheer pleasure of seeing enemies suffer.

◆ *Our friends may cause us to suffer.* Those we love best may break our hearts. What parent does not suffer when a child goes astray? Love intensifies suffering.

◆ *The kind of world we live in may cause suffering.* There are storms, floods, earthquakes, fires, accidents, and diseases. We cannot blame God. He made the world good and peaceful. Sin is to blame.

◆ *We may suffer for a cause.* Free men will die for cherished freedoms.

◆ *Suffering for Christ is the highest form of suffering.* This is more than persecution; this is voluntarily taking up one's cross. The apostle Paul suffered in a way vastly different from Simon of Cyrene. It may be that the highest joy comes through the sufferings for Christ that we could have avoided. The crosses that God would never thrust upon us but that we rejoicingly assume in deep anguish for His sake—these are the plus signs that point us upward to God.

Prayer: *Lord, give me staying power to persevere in hardship. I don't know why I suffering, but I must hold true.*

... Tie a Knot

Scripture: "And the God of all grace . . . after you have suffered a little while, will himself restore you and make you strong."

(1 Pet. 5:10, NIV)

I had to go to the business where she was working to tell her that her son had been killed in action halfway around the world. She sat in silence in the small room, too stunned to believe it, while I groped for words that would help. She was at the end of her rope.

I tried to minister to a trembling teenager whose father had suffered a mental collapse. His irrational actions had brought embarrassment to his family and friends. Kneeling in the corner of a lonely room, my young friend prayed for a father whom he desperately needed and who would never be the same again. That teen was at the end of his rope.

I sought to comfort a young woman whose home was burning to the ground. All her earthly possessions were going up in flames. There was no way to help, and she had no insurance. She was at the end of her rope.

A splendid young minister was caught in the crossfire of a church dispute and was asked to leave. How could he have done better? Why did it happen to him? Where would he go now? I had no answers. He was at the end of his rope.

Everyone comes to the end of his or her rope sooner or later. Isaiah did. Paul did. David did. Judas did. Likely at some point in our lives, you and I will too.

What should we do when we come to that bitter place? Judas took the cowardly, wrong way. David repented and found peace. Isaiah trusted God and soared like an eagle. Paul quit praying long enough to hear God say, "My grace is sufficient for thee: for my strength is made perfect in weakness" (2 Cor. 12:9). Why not let God take over? He never fails!

Prayer: *Father, I ask today that You will hold me in the midst of my misery and make me strong in my weakness.*

Finding the Way of Escape

Scripture: "Do not set foot on the path of the wicked or walk in the way of evil men."

(Prov. 4:14, NIV)

Here are some good methods to employ in resisting temptation:

◆ *Say no and mean it.* Use some self-discipline. Make up your mind to be victorious this time and every time beginning now. God can make you victorious only as you discipline yourself.

◆ *Do not toy with temptation.* Refuse to talk about it. Refuse to look at it. Refuse to let your mind dwell on it. Think immediately of God and His power to help you.

◆ *Get away from the tempting environment immediately.* Avoid the place, the job, the relationship, or the people who tempt you to sin. Refuse to view movies or television programs or to read books or magazines that incite you to do wrong. If you want to be pure, shun the impure.

◆ *Get busy at something else quickly.* Drive out the temptation by working with your hands, your mind, your tongue. Find some worthwhile activity to overcome the evil suggestion.

◆ *Keep close to Christian people.* Make your friends among the holy rather than the worldly, while you continue to witness to non-Christian friends and coworkers.

◆ *Read your Bible.* Memorize it, lean on it, underscore the helpful verses. Don't be ashamed of God's Word.

◆ *Pray immediately and often.* Pray anywhere and everywhere—while working, driving, playing. God will help you to overcome temptation. You can conquer.

Prayer: *Lord, always remind me that while I have no control over being tempted, I can avoid thoughts, situations, people, and desires that I know will harm me.*

Delays and Denials

Scripture: "I waited patiently for the LORD."
(Ps. 40:1, NIV)

What if God answered all our prayers immediately, right on the spot? Like the fabled King Midas, we would happily turn everything we touched to gold. But our happiness would sour as his did when he touched his lovely daughter and she became a golden statue and when his bread became slabs of gold that he could not eat.

God's delays and denials in answering our prayers are on purpose. He does not function as a cosmic bellhop who jumps at our every whim. True, God does have power to answer any prayer. But that power is overshadowed by His wisdom. He knows that it is often better if we do not get everything we want. Even a parent knows this about a child and denies that child accordingly. Love has a way of holding back as well as giving.

But it does seem that on occasion God takes His own good time in answering our prayers even after we have prayed about the matter. Why is this?

◆ Maybe He wants to improve and perfect our faith, as with Abraham, who was promised a son in his old age. Even after he received the promise, he had to wait for several years, getting constantly older. But patience in the delay strengthened Abraham's faith, and the promise eventually became reality.

◆ Maybe He wants to test our faith, as with Elijah, who kept praying on Mount Carmel while his servant made seven trips to look for a cloud. Elijah had to get his eyes off the conditions and believe with a pure faith before the smallest cloud arose on the horizon.

◆ Maybe God needs time to work on stubborn wills of indifferent people. Sometimes we pray through for the salvation of sinners who are not yet concerned about spiritual things. But the answer is a glorious victory. "The effectual fervent prayer of a righteous man availeth much" (James 5:16) if we "let patience have her perfect work" (1:4).

Prayer: *Father, give me patience to equal my expectation.*

When I Don't Feel Sure

Scripture: "On the evening of that day . . . the doors being shut . . . for fear of the Jews . . . Jesus came." (John 20:19, RSV)

When assurance is delayed and doubts come, you can find helpful lessons from the experiences of Mary Magdalene and Thomas as recorded in John 20.

◆ Remember Easter. When you don't feel full of faith, remember that Christ's resurrection is a fact. And remember that the fullness of the Holy Spirit was available to His disciples soon after Easter.

◆ Spend some time alone in your quest for certainty. Shut out the world. Talk to God, and let Him talk to you. Ask Him to help you find a helpful scripture, and listen as He speaks to you through it.

◆ Continue to be faithful in worship. The very day Thomas stayed away was the day Jesus came. Look what Thomas missed!

◆ Tell God about your doubts. He is skilled at handling them. Be openly frank before Him, tell Him that you doubt Him, and ask His help.

◆ Don't dwell in the doldrums. Have faith for a better day. The life of certainty and assurance is for you as much as for the most victorious person you ever knew. Expect defeat, and you will be defeated. Expect victory, and victory will come.

◆ Look for Him at the same place where you last saw Him. Mary last saw Him in the grave and returned to find Him nearby—alive.

◆ Put faith above feelings. It was not easy for Thomas nor for Mary Magdalene. But even they did not make it a daily ceremony to feel of His body to be sure. You, too, will come to know assurance, regardless of feelings and emotions.

Prayer: *Lord, give me new assurance when I have shut the doors of my spirit, mind, or faith.*

Detour from Downfall

Scripture: "Righteousness exalteth a nation: but sin is reproach to any people."

(Prov. 14:34)

While Thomas Jefferson was writing the Declaration of Independence, Edward Gibbon was writing *The Decline and Fall of the Roman Empire.* The new nation of America was being warned to prevent its collapse just as the Roman society had done. The historian's account of the nation that died 1,500 years ago reads like last night's newspaper. Here are his five reasons:

1. Their rapid increase of divorce
2. Their constant increase of taxation
3. Their mad craze for pleasure
4. Their building of gigantic armaments
5. Their downgrading of vital religion

Three of these are spiritual matters that greatly concern us as Christians. With a heritage that Rome never had, we are blindly taking the same tragic steps to the same ultimate oblivion.

1. *Their rapid increase of divorce.* Our liberalized divorce laws undermine the dignity and sanctity of the home. Legalized adultery is still adultery regardless of how our media condones and promotes it.

3. *Their mad craze for pleasure.* Were the Romans as mad for pleasure as we? Our fascination with base perversions, our national addiction of alcohol, our sports madness (which glorifies athletes), the corruption of our media . . . Do these things warn us?

5. *Their downgrading of vital religion.* When will we recall that our faith in God is our national foundation? When will we quit downgrading Jesus Christ and make place for vital religion in all that we do?

There is tragedy just ahead if we do not heed these warnings. History says so. God says so. But it's not too late to turn back to God.

Prayer: *Our Father, help us as a nation and as individuals to live in constant respect for Your will.*

You Won't Find It in Heaven

Scripture: "He will wipe away all tears . . . and there shall be no more death . . . sorrow . . . crying, nor pain." (Rev. 21:4, TLB)

Rev. 21 lists eight things that are missing in heaven:

◆ *"No more sea"* (v. 1). The sea signifies separation. There will be no farewells, no last good-byes to anyone. The sea also signifies restlessness, and all will be calm in heaven—no more storms.

◆ *"God shall wipe away all tears"* (v. 4). Can you imagine a place where there is no more sorrow, or crying? Wouldn't it be wonderful to live where everyone is always happy? Heaven is that place.

◆ *"Neither shall there be any more pain"* (v. 4) There will be no hospitals, no headaches, no heartaches. Can you visualize a world without suffering?

◆ *"No more death"* (v. 4). Heaven will have no graves. There will be no more screeching, fiery crashes on the highway, no silent vigils in funeral homes. Christ has conquered death.

◆ *"And I saw no temple"* (v. 22). Why is there no temple, no place to worship, no church building? Because worship is not localized there. All of heaven will be as one vast temple, and we will worship everywhere.

◆ *No sun in heaven* (v. 23). The glory of God will lighten it, and "the Lamb is the light thereof." Jesus is not only the Light of the world but also the Light of heaven.

◆ *"There shall be no night there"* (v. 25). Christ has no "shadow of turning," as the earth and sun do. Night represents gloom, despair, sin, and danger, but heaven is perpetual day.

◆ *No sin in heaven* (v. 27). There will be nothing that "defileth, neither whatsoever worketh abomination, or maketh a lie." Heaven is a sinless place for a sinless people.

Heaven will be heaven because of the things that are not there. I want to go there, don't you?

Prayer: *Thank You, Father, that heaven will be free of misery. We look forward already to being present with You.*

Communicating with God

Why Pray?

Scripture: "If you remain in me and my words remain in you, ask whatever you wish, and it will be given you."
(John 15:7, NIV)

One of the most effective tricks of Satan is to make us think that "just a little talk with Jesus makes it right." It simply is not true. There must be some big talks with Jesus. Long talks and regular talks too. And He must talk with us if we are to become mature and strong. There are at least four reasons Christians should pray:

◆ *Because prayer defeats Satan.* There is a powerful, cunning, deceptive, determined, and vicious devil. He is after you and me personally. The first step in dealing with the devil is prayer. And lots of it!

◆ *Because prayer puts us at God's disposal.* It make us as clay in the hands of the potter. It enables us to say, "Thy will be done." It brings us to the place of full surrender. Then with Isaiah we can say sincerely, "Here am I; send me" (6:8).

◆ *Because prayer puts God at our disposal.* This is not blasphemy. It is a blessed truth. Of course, God is not an errand boy to jump every time we make a request in prayer. But He has yielded to us the keys of the Kingdom. The power He has is available to those He can trust with it. Notice what Jesus said: "What things soever ye desire, when ye pray, believe that ye receive them, and ye shall have them" (Mark 11:24). "If ye abide in me, and my words abide in you, ye shall ask what ye will, and it shall be done unto you" (John 15:7). And James declared, "The effectual fervent prayer of a righteous man availeth much" (5:16). When we stay on our knees before God long enough and often enough, we will lay hold of the power of God.

◆ *Because of what prayer accomplishes.* Much gets done when much time is spent in prayer. There is growth in grace. There are blessings like showers upon the parched land. There is Christlikeness. And there are revivals!

Let's spend enough time on our knees so that we may walk tall and strong for Him and through Him!

Prayer: *Lord, give me "staying power" so that I will purpose to remain truly consistent in my prayer life.*

Rx for Empty Prayers

Scripture: "Therefore I tell you, whatever you ask for in prayer, believe that you have received it, and it will be yours."

(Mark 11:24, NIV)

Prayer means different things to different people at different times. To the child it may mean mumbling words that have no significance. To the new convert it may mean fellowship and strength. To the suffering Christian it may mean supplication. To the warrior it may mean intercession.

This means that prayer is both subjective and objective. Prayer helps the person who does the praying, and it also helps the one for whom prayer is made. It is true that prayer changes things, people, and even God. It also changes circumstances and conditions. Prayer may revolutionize individuals, revitalize groups, and redirect the course of history. It has been responsible for more changes in human and world affairs than any of us will ever know about this side of eternity.

But prayer itself is never enough. Even earnest prayer is not enough. Loud, long, and beautiful prayer is not enough. When we examine our lack of spiritual progress as individuals or as local churches, we see this. The missing element in prayer that makes it effective is *faith*.

Faith reaches up while we pray and takes hold of God's promises. Faith opens the channel and allows God's blessings to flow unhindered. Faith is the cable through which the heavenly power comes in high voltage. Without faith, prayer is nothing more than words.

Prayer: *Father in heaven, save me from empty prayers by filling me with a faith big enough to trust You.*

The Prayer Jesus Refused to Pray

Scripture: "I do not pray that thou shouldst take them out of the world, but that thou shouldst keep them from the evil one."

(John 17:15, RSV)

In the high-priestly prayer of our Lord (John 17) we find Jesus praying for many things for His disciples. He prayed for their keeping (vv. 11, 15), for their unity (vv. 11, 21-23), for their joy (v. 13), for their sanctification (vv. 17, 19), for their perfection (v. 23), for their final salvation (v. 24), for them to see God's glory (v. 24), and for them to have God's love in them (v. 26).

However, at one point in His prayer, Jesus stopped: "I pray not that thou shouldest take them out of the world" (v. 15). It was the prayer Jesus refused to pray. He could have prayed for them to be translated to heaven with Him. He could have locked arms with them, all stepping up on heaven's cloud and ascending together. They would have missed all the stonings, beatings, imprisonments, persecutions, and brutal deaths for His name's sake. But Christ would not allow it. He would not even pray for it.

Why did Jesus refuse to pray this prayer? Why did He go back to the splendors of heaven and leave them in this world of woe? Two reasons. *First,* they needed to stay here for their own good. They needed the trials and persecutions to strengthen their moral fiber and make them stand tall in a sinful world. *Second,* they needed to stay here because the world needed them. The world was in darkness, and they were light. The world was rotting, and they were salt. The world was in despair, and they represented hope. The world was without God, and they had God to offer. The world needed to hear what they had to say.

But our Lord assumed a certain special responsibility toward His disciples when He refused their immediate deliverance from this world. He obligated himself to give them the grace of inner cleansing and power that would enable this tiny group to turn the world right side up. Therefore Jesus prayed: "Sanctify them" (v. 17). And His prayer was answered (Acts 2:4). He also prayed this prayer for you (v. 20). Has Christ's prayer for you been answered? It can be today.

Prayer: *Lord, thank You for Your intercessory prayers.*
Help us to trust Your wisdom.

The Prayer Jesus Refused to Answer

Scripture: "The man . . . begged to go with [Jesus]. Jesus
did not let him, but said, 'Go home.'"
(Mark 5:18-19, NIV)

Legion was a victim of Satanism and demon possession. This wild man did not take kindly to civilization. He lived like a hunted animal, finding food and water in the strangest places. He slept alongside the decaying corpses in the caves and holes of the Decapolis cemetery, overlooking the placid waters of the blue Galilee. But there was nothing placid about the soul of Legion. Demons drove him to strange, unnatural things. Those who sought to restrain Legion were amazed to see him snap the chains and run shrieking defiantly among the tombs.

Then Jesus came. When the Master had surveyed the full scope of the situation, He spoke a simple command: "Come out of the man, thou unclean spirit" (Mark 5:8). A nightmare became a sunrise. The devils left. Legion came calmly to his feet and sat at His feet, healed in mind and cleansed of demon possession.

Later when Christ and His disciples were entering their ship to leave the country of the Gadarenes, Legion asked for permission to join them. He wanted to travel and witness with them. He wanted to be Exhibit A, the living proof of the power that Christ has over the devil. He wanted men everywhere to see him and to give God the glory. He wanted people to welcome the 13th apostle.

Jesus answered his prayer with a no. Instead of taking him along as a curious exhibit from a faraway place, Jesus sent Legion right back to his own family and acquaintances in Decapolis. He was operating on the theory that those who knew Legion "before" and "after" would be the most impressed.

The theory still works. The most effective witnessing begins at home. In Decapolis "all men did marvel" (v. 20). They still do when they see changed lives.

Prayer: *God, please help me to show the real difference between the "before" and "after" You came into my life.*

Praying Faith over Fear

Scripture: "So I turned to the Lord God and pleaded with him in prayer and petition." (Dan. 9:3, NIV)

If a person is to pray as Daniel prayed, he must live as Daniel lived. The prayer he prayed in chapter 9 was not the product of the moment. It was an overflow of the years. Note what Daniel was doing through these years of his captivity.

◆ *He was cultivating some convictions.* The first glimpse of this is in Dan. 1:8. "Daniel purposed in his heart that he would not defile himself" with the king's meat or wine. Daniel knew what he believed and refused to compromise. Convictions are costly, but they pave the way for power in prayer.

◆ *He was paying attention to what God had to say.* He kept listening to the voice of God. Because there was little of the written Word of God, Daniel had to pay close attention. God helped Daniel find the answer to some dreams and visions simply because he listened. Many Christians would pray better if they listened better.

◆ *He was guarding his heart against selfishness.* His successes did not turn his head with a show of pride. He was humble in his promotions. He was selfless in his dealings with others. He was never haughty or deceptive. He never thought of himself as an outstanding success.

◆ *He was guarding his heart against fear.* Not always was Daniel placed in positions of security. Once it was the lions' den. Most people would panic there! But if Daniel was afraid, the lions never knew it. As a man of courage and conviction, Daniel possessed more faith than fear.

◆ *He was always practicing the art of prayer.* With him it was a habit: three times a day on his knees with the window open. But more than a habit, prayer was a way of life. No wonder Gabriel paid Daniel a visit.

More of us could pray as Daniel prayed if we would live as Daniel lived. Even one of us could move a nation Godward as he did. Will you be that one?

Prayer: *O God, make me a Daniel-like Christian, purposeful in my devotion and consistent in my prayer.*

Don't Be Afraid to Pray It

Scripture: "Our Father in heaven . . . your will be done."
(Matt. 6:9-10, NIV)

Our secret prayers usually have three faults: short, cold, and spasmodic. Yet, prayer doesn't have to be long and ornate to be effective.

Our Lord's prayer is the apex praying of all recorded communion with God. Four words of this passage are the most important words any person can possibly pray: "Thy will be done."

Doing God's will comes before asking for bread. It is not wrong to pray for life's necessities: food, health, work. It may not be wrong to ask for certain other temporal things. But God's will must ever be first and final.

"Thy will be done" is both a passive and an active prayer. Passively we resign ourselves to His will, whether the death of a loved one or the second coming of our Lord. But to pray "Thy will be done" may also mean that I must give more than a tithe, that I must witness to my coworkers, that I must teach a Sunday School class, or that I must be a pastor or a missionary.

Are we afraid to pray it? Jesus shuddered and sweated when He prayed these four words again at midnight Thursday before His crucifixion. But He was afraid *not* to pray them.

Is His will being done in *you*, *"in earth*, as it is in heaven"? Don't hesitate to pray the most important prayer in the Bible: "Thy will be done." And don't hesitate to act upon it.

Prayer: *Father, do as You please in my life. I pray this in Jesus' name.*

When a Nation Prays

Scripture: "O LORD, God of Israel, there is no God like you in heaven above or on earth below."

(1 Kings 8:23, NIV)

I recall how as a very small boy I came from playing in the backyard, calling for Mother's attention. But Mother was not in the kitchen. I searched upstairs, quietly tiptoeing from room to room. At last I found her kneeling beside her bed in prayer. Quickly and quietly I closed the door and went back to my play. But I never forgot that scene of my mother kneeling. I dared not disturb her while she was having audience with the King of Kings.

It is a splendid and wonderful thing to see a Christian kneeling. Corporate prayer at our churches and at large evangelistic crusades inspires us as we see hundreds or even thousands kneeling together.

Wouldn't it be grand to see an entire nation kneeling together in praise and supplication to God? This has happened in history when the people prayed together and when they were led in a common prayer, such as when Solomon dedicated the Temple. And the time will come when "every knee shall bow, and every tongue confess" in that great day of the Lord.

Every nation on earth would do well to set aside a day of prayer and supplication with soul-searching. Though we may never see our entire nation follow this pattern, we must each begin with our own lifestyle of prayer.

God is still God, and we are still accountable to Him. Let us begin today in our individual prayers, at our family altars, in our local churches, and throughout the world to bombard heaven's portals through the avenue of prayer. It is our only hope.

Prayer: *Jesus, I kneel before You in my heart to proclaim You as my personal Savior and Lord.*

The Guidebook

Scripture: "Your word is a lamp to my feet and
a light for my path."   (Ps. 119:105, NIV)

J. Wilbur Chapman gives us these insights to the study of God's Word in His classic book, *The Secret of Bible Study.*

◆ *Study it through.* Never begin a day without mastering a verse.

◆ *Pray it in.* Never leave your Bible until the passage you have studied is a part of your very being.

◆ *Put it down.* Write the thought God gives you in the margin of your Bible or notebook.

◆ *Work it out.* Live the truth you receive throughout the day.

◆ *Pass it on.* Tell somebody what you have learned.

These quotes about the Bible remind us of its worth to people everywhere throughout history.

"I have known ninety-five great men of the world in my time, and of these, eighty-seven were followers of the Bible."—W. E. Gladstone

"I am profitably engaged in reading the Bible. Take all of this Book upon reason that you can, and the balance by faith, and you will live and die a better man."—Abraham Lincoln

"Believe me, sir, never a night goes by, be I ever so tired, but I read the Word of God before I go to bed."—Douglas MacArthur

"It is impossible to rightly govern the world without God and the Bible. He is worse than an infidel who does not read his Bible and acknowledge his obligation to God."—George Washington

"The Bible is the best Book in the world."—John Adams

"I have always said, and always will say, that the studious perusal of the Sacred Volume will make better citizens, better fathers, better husbands. The Bible makes the best people in the world."—Thomas Jefferson

"If God is a reality and you are an immortal soul, what are you doing with your Bible shut?"—Herrick Johnson

Prayer: *O, Lord, I humbly affirm Your precious Word
as my guide throughout all of life.*

The Divine Treasure Hunt

Scripture: "Do your best to present yourself to God as one approved, a workman who does not need to be ashamed and who correctly handles the word of truth."
(2 Tim. 2:15, NIV)

◆ *Take time.* If we can find time for eating, socializing, and relaxing, we can find time for God's Word. Meditation is not a hurried act.

◆ *Go slowly.* There is no value in skimming over several chapters at a time. It is better to spend 15 minutes on one word or one verse, drinking in its richness, than to cover a lot of territory without getting the lasting benefit.

◆ *Dig deep.* There is no place for shallow thinking in Bible reading. God's Word is so vast that it is possible to keep digging in the same place for a long time with rewarding success.

◆ *Run references.* Compare scripture with scripture—thought with thought—word with word. Use a reference Bible. Don't be afraid to mark your Bible with underlines, marginal notes, and personal comments.

◆ *Be curious.* Find out who is writing and to whom. Discover when, what, why, and under what circumstances. Look into backgrounds. Study personalities. Probe character. Find out what other people have said about the passage at hand.

◆ *Be reverent.* The Bible is the Word of God, not of humans. Believe what you read . . . not because you understand all there is to know, but because God said it. In all your digging and searching, do not be critical of divine authority. God's thoughts are above ours. But they are still God's.

◆ *Be obedient.* Take it personally. Obey what you see in print and what you sense in your heart. Pause to pray while you study. Avoid the purely intellectual. Ask God to apply His Word to your heart and lift you to a higher level of living.

Prayer: *Lord, I reverence Your Word enough to read and study it. Help me also to obey and proclaim it.*

Book of Books

Scripture: "For everything . . . was . . . written to teach us, so that through endurance and encouragement of the Scriptures we might have hope."

(Rom. 15:4, NIV)

The Bible is the Book of books. It is not only the Book above and beyond all other books but also is itself a Book of many books. While there is unity, there is also variety. While it is one Book, yet it is many books. This fact itself is one of the very strong arguments for its divine inspiration.

The Bible has books of laws. Some of the laws were ceremonial and temporary; others were ethical and moral, and thus eternal. Some passed away when Christ came; others were fortified and strengthened by His coming. He came not to destroy the moral and spiritual laws but to fulfill them.

The Bible has books of history in both the Old Testament and the New Testament. There are histories of God's dealings with His people and of their responses. There is the history of the establishment of the Church.

The Bible has books of wisdom and instruction, reading like a parent talking to a child or like a pastor counseling those who are seeking the right way.

The Bible has books of praises. There are songs for all occasions and for all circumstances . . . gladness, joy, hope, and despair. Some sing of yearning for a better country; some sing of deliverance and redemption.

The Bible has books of correspondence. There are letters to young churches and to young Christians. And it has books of prophecy, too, pointing us to events that will shortly come to pass. Thank God for this divine Library—the Book of books!

Prayer: *Your Word is varied, Father. Teach me from all of its pages how to live a faithful and fruitful life.*

Back to the Book

Scripture: "I have hidden your word in my heart that I might not sin against you."

(Ps. 119:11, NIV)

The current moral decay of our society can be traced more directly to the neglect of God's Word than to any point of our modern compass. We have lost our way as a civilization because the individual, the family, and the nation as a whole have neglected the Bible.

Often Christians ask, "How can I best study the Bible?" May I offer some suggestions:

◆ *Individual and personal Bible study is the place to begin.* It must be a do-it-yourself project, and it must not be delayed. Begin today. Reading guides are available. These will guide you through the Bible in a year. A topical study of the Bible could be made the second year of your serious and systematic examination of God's Word.

Or, having read the entire Bible through consecutively, you could then reread certain books of the Bible with great profit. Never be afraid to mark your Bible. Always read it with a colored pencil, pen, or highlight marker in hand. It's good to make notes in the margin too. Wide-margin Bibles are available especially for this.

◆ *Family Bible study is of almost equal importance.* Someone must take the lead in this, so why not you? Use devotional material along with Bible reading, followed by prayer. Give the exercise variety and life. Do it at the same time each day as a regular part of your schedule.

◆ *Group Bible study is also very important.* If there is no group in your community, organize a group of your own. Weekly meetings of women, men, young people, or couples are proving very helpful. Materials are available for group studies. Keep the meeting saturated with prayer and free from gossip.

Above all, become a student of the Bible. It is God's Word!

Prayer: *Lord, because the Bible is Your Word, I respect it enough to study it, memorize it, and keep it in my mind and heart.*

Bible Basics

Scripture: "For Ezra had devoted himself to the study and observance of the Law of the LORD."

(Ezra 7:10, NIV)

Digging into the Word of God is work, but it is pleasant work. It takes time, tools, curiosity, patience, and insight. Here are a few simple ways to get at it:

◆ *Who?* Who is talking? To whom? About whom? In whose presence? Identify each character in detail. Give names. What do these names mean? Learn all you can about the people in the Scripture.

◆ *Where?* Where does this passage take place? Name the city, town, river, lake, mountain, valley, or forest. Locate the places on a map. What is there today? What changes have been made?

◆ *When?* Did this occur before or after the life of Christ? Exactly what year? What was going on at that time in Jerusalem? In Rome? In Babylon? In Egypt? In Europe? Name some contemporary figures in history at that date. How many years before (or after) Noah? Abraham? David? Moses? Isaiah? Jesus?

◆ *By whom?* Who wrote or spoke this passage? What was the occasion? How sure are we of authorship? Find some interesting facts about the author and the occasion.

◆ *Why?* Why was this passage written or spoken? What prompted it? What was the purpose of the passage?

◆ *What?* What is the author trying to tell us? What does he hope to accomplish in this message? What is there in it for us today? What deductions, implications, or instructions are meant for us today? How can we apply the lesson to ourselves?

◆ *How?* How can my life benefit from this passage? How can I better myself? How does God expect me to act after this study?

Prayer: *Father, help me to pay the price of being a diligent student of Your Word.*

Living to Please God

Is God Impressed?

Scripture: "And what does the LORD require . . . ? To act justly and to love mercy and to walk humbly."
(Mic. 6:8, NIV)

In our image-conscious culture, people seem obsessed with impressing their coworkers, their rivals, their friends, their enemies, their bosses, and their families. They cultivate an impressive image through the clothes they wear, the cars they drive, the friends they seek, and the places they go.

Some people are attempting to impress God through externals that seem shallow, such as long prayers, faithful giving, service, and ritual. Entire congregations mistakenly seek divine favor by engaging in extreme ritualism, extreme emotionalism, extreme legalism, even extreme fanaticism. But these things do not impress God.

When we give generously merely for prestige or self-satisfaction, God points to the ultimate sacrifice of the poor widow who gave only two coins but all that she had. When we pray dramatically merely for great oratory, God reminds us of groanings that cannot be spoken in words.

This is not to say that God is unimpressed by the finer qualities of our worship. But He is looking behind the action to weigh the motive. He is always impressed more by the reason than by the deed.

In our humanity, we are ever near the danger zone of substituting the superficial for the spiritual, of going through the motions instead of seeking His Spirit, emphasizing the ritual and neglecting the real worship.

It's time to get tired of the ordinary and get hungry for the extraordinary. God is impressed by a holy sincerity that strips us of the superficial and opens our hearts to His indwelling fullness! Hosea reminds us that the desires of divinity are a steadfast love rather than a lovely ritual.

Prayer: *Lord, teach me the basics! Never let me stray in word, thought, or deed.*

Contemporary or Traditional

Scripture: "The priests could not continue to minister because of the cloud, for the glory of the LORD filled the house."

(2 Chron. 5:14, NEB)

Worship is not identical from one part of the country to another or even from church to church. New forms of worship are attempting to recapture the scriptural pattern of the true worship of God. Although the forms of true worship are flexible, the ingredients of worship are constant if holy results are to be achieved. Look at God's pattern in 2 Chron. 5.

◆ *Human involvement* (vv. 11-12). The priests and the Levites together with their sons were involved. People still need to be involved in public worship if there is to be a meaningful moment with the Lord.

◆ *Music* (vv. 12-13). There was joyful singing! Multiple musical instruments were used in God's house—an orchestra! What a happy occasion!

◆ *Unity* (v. 13). They "were as one" just as on the Day of Pentecost. Fragmented, divided Christians cannot have productive worship.

◆ *Gratitude* (v. 13). Thanksgiving is basic to worship. Gratitude of the heart must be expressed openly, or it will atrophy.

◆ *Praise* (v. 13). Whether one at a time or in unison, praise is imperative. And like gratitude, it must be both experienced and expressed.

◆ *Divine presence* (v. 14). "The glory of the LORD had filled the house." When involvement in worship, singing, unity, and gratitude exist, God's presence can be expected. And there is no substitute!

◆ *A take-home truth from God* (7:12-14). Solomon had a word from the Lord that lingered with him long after the worship service was over. True worship never ends with the benediction. There is always a new truth to be lived.

Prayer: *Lord, when I come to church on Sunday, show me Your presence and teach me my response.*

Preaching like Peter

Scripture: "But Peter . . . raised his voice and declared, . . . 'Give heed to my words.'"

(Acts 2:14, NASB)

Peter's sermon in Acts does not compare with certain philosophical pulpit utterances, nor with modern psychological approaches, nor with homiletical treatises that are sometimes read or recited by sophisticated preachers today. But his sermon is a pattern for holy preaching, for it was . . .

◆ A *scripture-packed preaching.* Much of what he said was quoted from the Bible or read from it as he preached. God's Word must still have primacy in our preaching if it is to be effective.

◆ A *Christ-centered preaching.* Almost one-half of this recorded sermon pointed to Jesus. Holy preaching always magnifies Him. Stories, theories, and opinions must give way to Christ and His message.

◆ A *Spirit-anointed preaching.* Peter honored the Holy Spirit. His opening remarks pointed to the fact that the Holy Spirit had come according to prophecy. Spiritual preaching always magnifies the work of the Holy Spirit.

◆ A *testimony-experience preaching.* Much of Peter's sermon was a personal witness of what happened in his own heart (v. 40). Effective preachers have the undeniable certainty of personal experience in their preaching.

◆ A *warning-exhortation preaching.* He called the people to repentance and to a changed life. He warned them with caring emotion.

◆ A *"thou art the man" preaching.* Peter pointed to their bloody hands. Effective preaching must always rebuke sin and face sinners with their guilt.

◆ A *conviction-producing preaching.* Peter was not seeking revenge nor trying to make people angry. Yet he preached for a decision. His sermon climaxed when they were pricked in their hearts and asked how to be saved.

◆ *A drawing-the-net preaching.* Holy Spirit-filled preaching will produce converts.

Pray for your pastor as he or she stands to preach this Sunday. It is an awesome responsibility.

Prayer: *God, fill my pastor with Your words as he [or she] preaches, and give him [or her] converts for his [or her] labor.*

When the Cheering Stopped

Scripture: "The crowds that went ahead of [Jesus]
and those that followed shouted,
'Hosanna to the Son of David!'"
(Matt. 21:9, NIV)

How thrilling it must have been to see the crowd acclaim Jesus
on that first Palm Sunday morning when our Lord came riding into
Jerusalem. Some of the multitudes went before Him, clearing the
way and spreading their cloaks on the ground as a cushion for the
feet of the beast upon which Jesus rode. Others cut down the branches of trees and decorated the street ahead of Him. Then as our Lord
came riding along on the colt, the multitudes cheered, rejoiced, and
wept for joy. Loudly they cried out their acclaim of His divinity:
"Hosanna to the son of David: Blessed is he that cometh in the name
of the Lord; Hosanna in the highest" (Matt. 21:9). It was their finest
hour, even if the finest hour of Jesus had not yet come.

But these Palm Sunday followers did not stick. By nine o'clock
Friday morning they had all run for cover. It's even possible that
some joined in the hoarse blasphemy, "Crucify Him!"

What happened to those Palm Sunday followers? Why did their
blood run thin and pale within five days? Why were they never an-
chored? Were they misled by the "Dreamer"? Did they fail to count
the cost of discipleship? Did they act on the enthusiasm of the moment rather than the conviction of a lifetime?

The question must come closer home. How many of us waver in
our allegiance to Christ when the circumstances turn grim? How
fickle will we be when the pressure is on? What can help us stand
firm in our devotion to Christ? Jesus Christ is the Anchor; the Holy
Spirit enables us to live the disciplined life. Can He count on you?

Prayer: *Lord, please save me from wavering like the Palm Sunday
crowds. Enable me to trust You for more than Your miracles and parables.*

Christ and the Cobra

Scripture: "For sin shall not be your master."
(Rom. 6:14, NIV)

Years ago a missionary in the Orient was visiting a man in his humble hut. As they sat talking, one of the children of the Oriental brought a saucer of food and cautiously placed it in the middle of the room near a hole in the crude floor. The missionary inquired as to the meaning of this, and the man replied, "Be patient a moment, and you shall understand." Presently there was a gentle rustling sound in the direction of the hole in the floor, and the ugly head of a deadly cobra snake appeared for his daily feast from the saucer. The man explained, "King Cobra lives here."

So it is with humankind. There is a king cobra called sin living and ruling in every Christless heart. "All have sinned, and come short of the glory of God" (Rom. 3:23). "There is none that doeth good, no, not one" (v. 12). "All we like sheep have gone astray" (Isa. 53:6). The human race is "filled with all unrighteousness, fornication, wickedness, covetousness, maliciousness; full of envy, murder, debate, deceit, malignity; whisperers, backbiters, haters of God, despiteful, proud, boasters, inventors of evil things, disobedient to parents" (Rom. 1:29-30). How deadly is the venom of sin!

But Christ came to cope with the cobra. He died to take away the sting of sin, which is eternally fatal. We need not be mastered by sin. Although every man is born with an enemy within, all who come to Christ may be transformed, gloriously delivered, wonderfully redeemed. Let Christ rule in your heart.

Prayer: *Thank You, God, that Christ is greater than our personal sin. I yield my life to You for cleansing.*

Saying No to God

Scripture: "And the LORD God commanded . . . , 'you must not eat from the tree'" (Gen. 2:16-17, NIV). "The man said, . . . 'I ate it'" (3:12, NIV).

Man, fresh from the hand of his Creator, was placed in Eden's glad garden. God had given him certain duties and responsibilities. Man had sweet fellowship with his Creator daily. There were God-given permissions and prohibitions. God's authority was clear, and His laws had their penalties and rewards.

Then came temptation. Satan suggested that God did not mean exactly what He had said, that it was right to disobey just this once, that disobedience would not bring awful consequences as God had warned. And the temptation was sharpened by desire. The forbidden looked so appetizing! The true nature of sin did not show up with all its heartache, remorse, regret, and blackness. The temptation was a veneer of sin's allurement.

So the first pair yielded. They said a deliberate *no* to God and a deliberate *yes* to self. It was holiness rejected and sin embraced. It was finite humans spurning the infinite God. It was the creature in rebellion against the Creator.

But this rebellion against God had its awful consequences. First came guilt and condemnation. Then came broken fellowship with God. Eden was lost. Work became a drudgery. The earth and the elements were cursed. The race was plunged headlong into heartache. The fresh soil was stained with blood and scarred by the first grave when brother murdered brother. And this rebellion has brought itself to a full tide today. Just look about you for its increasing evidences.

But there is hope. Look above you for the cure of the curse. Christ stands ready to forgive. We must accept His authority and respond to Him in complete obedience daily.

Prayer: *God, teach me the simplest thing of all. You are God, and I am me. You made the rules, and I obey. Help me to keep it straight.*

The Seven-headed Dragon

Scripture: "Beware! Don't always be wishing for what you don't have. For real life and real living are not related to how rich we are." (Luke 12:15, TLB)

Greed is perhaps the root sin of all sins. It is the twisted desire that produces pleasing but poisonous flowers that pollute all of life. Notice how greed devours the good and the holy in life through covetousness.

◆ *Pleasure.* God's way is the pleasant and pleasurable path, but greed turns clean pleasure into sour sin through thirst for illicit sex, life-destroying drugs, forbidden relationships, and other unholy indulgences.

◆ *Possessions.* Money, cars, clothes, furniture, houses, lands, properties, and investments are not wrong of themselves. It is not what a person *has* that destroys him; it is what *has* the person. Are you greedy for things? Do they possess you?

◆ *Popularity.* Everyone wants and needs friends. But there is danger that one will pay too much to be accepted.

◆ *Position.* It is good to enlarge your scope of usefulness as a leader. But beware of bitterness if you are not given a position of leadership or prestige. In God's kingdom, there is plenty of work that needs to be done. Jesus said that the highest position was being a servant.

◆ *Prestige.* It is a comfortable feeling to be in the "in crowd." But not all are, and the membership is often temporary. It was for Jesus and for the leaders in the Early Church, and it has been for spiritual people through the years. It is better to be in Christ's inner circle.

◆ *Power.* It is good to influence people in the right direction, but it is a sin to seek power for a selfish purpose. Power in the hands of unworthy people is a dangerous thing in any organization, including the church.

◆ *Praise.* Knowing that one has done a task well brings satisfaction. But serving only to receive praise negates the good that is done.

God's cleansing Holy Spirit is the cure for covetousness.

Prayer: *God, please save me from the snare of wanting more than I need. Help me to learn contentment with what I have.*

The Most Expensive Item

Scripture: "For Christ died for sins once for all, the righteous for the unrighteous, to bring you to God." (1 Pet. 3:18, NIV)

Sin is the most expensive thing in the world. It cost God the perfect, eternal peace that had always been His. It cost heaven the harmony it had always known before Lucifer started the very first war. It necessitated the creation of hell. It disturbed the Holy Trinity. It cost heaven her rarest and most perfect Jewel. It cost Jesus His heavenly splendor. It sent our Lord into the earthly limitations of a human body and a sinful world. It broke that eternal fellowship with the Father for one dark moment at Golgotha. It loaded Him with burdens that He did not deserve and accomplished His death in spite of His innocence.

Sin cost the world its first and only Eden and turned it into a place of chaos, floods, thorns, storms, and earthquakes. It wrote the pages of history in blood. Sin has scarred the face of the glove with ugly graves. Sin built every hospital and every prison. Sin is to blame for every broken home, every broken body, every broken heart, every broken life.

Sin has made man a beast of burden, loaded down by guilt. Sin has erected barriers, broken fellowship, and split churches, families, and friends. Sin has caused men to hate, to fight, to lower themselves to the level of the animal. Sin has brought guilt, remorse, and despair, taking away sunshine, peace, and hope. Sin has blighted character and destroyed self-respect.

Is it any wonder that God hates sin as He does? Yet He has given His Son to die in our place to provide forgiveness and reconciliation. Live above sin through the power of His Holy Spirit. That power is available to you today.

Prayer: *Lord, thank You for dying for us though we were sinners and for bringing us to God.*

Just Keep Moving

Scripture: "But if we walk in the light, as [God] is in the light . . . the blood of Jesus, his Son, purifies us from all sin."
(1 John 1:7, NIV)

When we were boys, my brother and I often kept the tractor running day and night to accomplish our work while the weather was cooperative. Many dark nights found us moving up and down the fields with lanterns tied to the front of the tractor. These lights were so ineffective that we were able to see only the immediate furrow about five feet ahead. We made it a practice to keep moving with the light we had.

And it worked. Although we did not have light to see the distant trees and the houses on the far horizon, we had a little light; so we kept moving. All we really needed to know was that we were in the furrow. When the corner came, we were ready for it because we had seen it five feet in advance. By morning it was surprising to find that we had plowed a considerable strip of land—never seeing more than five feet ahead at any one time as we circled that 200-acre tract.

"Walking in the light" is an expression that we hear frequently. It simply means that in the Christian life, the people of God keep moving ahead as far as they can see. It means that we do not quit because we can see only a little way. It means that as we walk, the way is made clear for the next step. We trust God for the unknown future, but at the same time we are obedient to the known present.

Volumes have been written and scores of sermons have been preached about knowing the will of God. Christians everywhere are instructed continually how they may find God's guidance in the tomorrows of their lives. This is good. But have we said enough about doing the will of God as we now know His will? If we do the will of God as we presently know it, then it will be easier to see the next step after that.

Prayer: *Lord, help me to keep walking—to be faithful on my daily journey and never to stray out of relationship with You.*

Penetrate or Perish

Scripture: "You are the salt of the earth."
(Matt. 5:13, NIV)

Hog killing day always filled our childish lives with the unusual, the unexpected, the exciting. Routine farm and home duties were pushed aside. New adventures called. Experts at butchering were always venturing advice. But work spoiled it all! One of the distasteful tasks assigned to me was rubbing sugar-cured salt into the freshly trimmed hams. For hours on end I would press the brown grains by the handful into the bulky chunks. My frequent pauses were prodded with advice: "The salt in the bag will never help the ham in the smokehouse . . . Rub the salt into the meat, or the ham will spoil and the salt will waste away." We proved it months later when each breakfast plate was loaded with bright red slabs of tasty ham, circled by halos of red ham gravy and flanked by hot, brown-backed biscuits and ribbon cane syrup.

I recall that advice today: "The salt in the bag will never help the ham in the smokehouse." The salt must make contact with the meat, or both will be wasted. Christians whom Jesus called salt will never save the world by shutting themselves away from the world. God did not design the Church to remain behind closed doors, rather to penetrate the world to save it.

The Church in her weakest hour is always isolated from the world. She is removed from the reality of rampant sin, crouched behind the closed doors of ecclesiasticism, denominationalism, sectarianism, ritualism. And the Church in her finest hour is always penetrating the world as Peter penetrated the city council, as Paul penetrated Philippi, as Luther penetrated Worms, as Wesley penetrated England and America. With salty Christians, it is penetrate or perish.

Prayer: *Let my life, like salt, penetrate my world. Lord, help me to make a difference today.*

Learning to Live in Faith

Graduating in Faith

Scripture: "I am pressing toward the goal."
(Phil. 3:14, GOODSPEED)

Paul outlines some of the main qualities of mature faith in Philippians:

◆ *Detachment.* Abraham separated himself from his prosperous surroundings and headed for the heights of Canaan. As faith matures, the things of this world take less priority in our lives.

◆ *Attachment.* Fully grown faith takes hold of the spiritual. More and more we live in the light of God. Faith fastens us to Him.

◆ *Contentment.* Those who live to gratify the five senses are never content. But faith goes beyond feeling, fixing our affections on things above. That inner "all is well" feeling comes with mature faith.

◆ *Accomplishment.* A mature faith not only abstains from forbidden things but accomplishes positive action for God. The Scripture says that the faithful "subdued kingdoms, wrought righteousness, obtained promises, stopped the mouths of lions, quenched the violence of fire, escaped the edge of the sword, out of weakness were made strong, waxed valiant in fight, turned to flight the armies of the aliens" (Heb. 11:33-34).

◆ *Certainty.* Doubts are put away. The perplexities of life, which are difficult to understand, are committed to a higher wisdom. Mature faith is not content to flounder. It has arrived at a glorious assurance and has driven down a stake. With certainty, John said, "We do know that we know" (1 John 2:3).

◆ *Purpose.* Faith knows what it wants, why it wants it, and where it is going. Unlike the shotgun with its scatter-load, faith is a high-powered rifle with one bullet zeroed in on the target. It is a "this one thing I do" aim (Phil. 3:13).

◆ *Optimism.* Mature faith and optimism cannot be divorced. Falling bombs cannot take away our confidence in the ultimate outcome. We have poise and peace because we are God's. He is still there, and knowing it, we take fresh courage!

Prayer: *God, give me the courage never to give up
in my pursuit of Your will.*

Touching, Believing, Receiving

Scripture: "Before all the people she explained why she had touched him and how she had been instantly cured."
(Luke 8:47, NEB)

Luke 8 tells us that He was on His way to heal a dying child when detained by an unknown woman who touched Him in faith. That divine touch is still available to us.

◆ *Believe that Jesus is accessible.* He is never too busy to listen and to help. He desires to be interrupted by our cry for aid. He is always delighted when we bring our needs to Him.

◆ *Cast off the fear of past failures.* Luke's story tells us that the woman Jesus healed had lived for 12 years with an illness that physicians could not cure (8:43). What a record of failure she had to overcome! We must bring our past failures as well as our present needs to Him.

◆ *Make contact with Christ in spite of people.* The woman had to press her way into His presence before she could touch Him. People cannot keep us from Christ's blessings unless we allow them to quench our faith.

◆ *Touch Christ in faith.* Many jostled Jesus that day without receiving His blessing. But this woman was healed because she touched *in faith.* She reached through people and touched just the border of His robe. Her faith took hold of divine power in that moment.

◆ *Make public confessions when you touch Him.* Luke took three verses (45-47), more than half of the story, to show how eager Jesus was for the woman to identify herself. Public testimony is for our good and His glory.

When we touch Christ in faith, we get a double blessing (v. 48). The woman was not only healed but also comforted by Christ. She received healing *and* peace. Her way was the same old way, but *she* was different. No one can be the same after touching Him.

What of your past failures? Why not press your way into the presence of the Master and touch Him in faith? He is nearer than you know.

Prayer: *Lord, give me the faith of this woman who forgot her fears and failures long enough to touch and trust You.*

When My Faith Seems Anemic

Scripture: "Faith comes from hearing the message, and the message is heard through the word of Christ."

(Rom. 10:17, NIV)

The little boy in Sunday School defined faith as "believing something that isn't so." Before we toss his definition out as a total fallacy, perhaps we should hunt for a better one.

More accurately, faith is dependence upon the honesty of another person. It is believing that God will do what He said He would do. It is much like trust: relying upon the truth of a promise.

Why do some people have strong faith while others scoff? Perhaps we should recognize certain laws by which we are able to exercise faith.

◆ *Faith is choked by condemnation.* If people disobey, they strangle their faith because they are under a cloud of guilt. Repeated disobedience may pave the way to ultimate apostasy.

◆ *Faith is based on obedience to God's will.* This includes His written will and His will personally revealed beyond the written page. The more we follow the will of God, the surer and brighter our faith. Obedience lifts faith.

◆ *Faith is subject to the authority of God's Word.* If we reject the Bible as God's Word, we have no basis upon which to exercise faith. However, if we accept God's Word as true and meaningful, then faith takes hold.

◆ *Faith is often measured by one's knowledge of God's Word.* The person who has never heard has a hard time believing. The giants of faith about us today are the ones who spend much time reading and rejoicing in God's Word.

Prayer: *Lord, renew my hunger for Your Word so that my faith may increase.*

Willing to Believe

Scripture: "I do believe; help me overcome my unbelief!"
(Mark 9:24, NIV)

◆ *Faith resides in the will—not in the intellect or the emotions.*
The person who says, "I cannot believe," is really saying, "I will not
believe." To demand complete answers to all intellectual and emotional questions before one is willing to believe is to eliminate faith en-
tirely. This makes Christianity utterly humanistic and materialistic.

◆ *Faith is a willingness to believe now and understand later.* It
is a willingness to accept God's conclusions without knowing all the
secret steps God has taken to arrive at those conclusions.

◆ *Faith is a willingness to obey now and see the results later.*
Faith must be active; we must not only believe but also act on the basis of what we believe. We do not need to know it all; we need only
to trust, to believe, and to act as a believer.

◆ *Faith is intellectual and spiritual humility.* We believe in
Someone who knows more than we know. Admitting that God
knows more than we know makes us trust in His wisdom, power,
and love. It gives us strength and certainty in the process.

◆ *Faith is not intellectual dishonesty.* It is not "believing something that isn't so" or denying that our own doubts trouble us. Faith
helps us to doubt our own doubts and believe our beliefs. Remember
the old saying that urges us to put all our troubles in a box, sit on the
lid, and laugh? Let's put all our doubts in a box and *trust God!* Then
our souls will rejoice.

Prayer: *Lord, sometimes my faith wavers. Help me rely
so completely on You that my faith will never vanish.*

Closed to Unbelievers

Scripture: "And they spread among the Israelites a bad report."

(Num. 13:32, NIV)

God promised Israel that Canaan would be theirs, yet a whole generation died before they entered. Why?

◆ *Israel kept threatening to go back to Egypt.* They did not have the faith to face up to God's promises. There was a certain security in slavery that they didn't have now. And there was a challenge in being free that they hesitated to face. They should have considered retreat impossible.

◆ *They failed to quit complaining when they left Egypt.* They complained because they had no water, because the water was bitter, because they had no bread, because they had no meat, because Moses prayed too long on the mountain. Complaining people are not good cadidates for the Promised Land.

◆ *They had a grasshopper complex.* The giants of Canaan were so large that they considered themselves to be mere grasshoppers by comparison. Though they were no longer slaves, something of the slave complex stuck with them. They experienced carnal cowardice. We should never brag of our own might, but we can all feel a security when we have God at our side.

◆ *Their plans were not large enough to include God.* They set down some cold figures without any warm faith, and their conclusion was, "It can't be done." So they voted to stay where they were, and they stayed there 40 years and lost a whole generation. A little faith in a big God would have opened Canaan for them. It will do the same for us today.

Prayer: *O God, I am only one person, but give me faith equal to my task.*

Cultivating a
Christian Family

Chosen to Parent

Scripture: "Each year his mother made him a little robe
and took it to him."

(1 Sam. 2:19, NIV)

When God gets ready to bring a great man into the world, He often looks about for a good, noble woman through whom to give that gift. Is it any wonder that Wesley's mother was a woman of patience, piety, and strength? Or that Augustine's mother spent a great deal of time in intense intercessory prayer? Or that Lincoln's mother exacted a pledge from young Abe that he would never touch liquor or tobacco? On the contrary, it is not surprising that Nero's mother was a murderess.

At a critical turning point in Israel's history, God needed a special kind of man. He sought out a special kind of woman to be his mother. The mother was Hannah. The man was Samuel. Samuel came through a woman of deepest consecration, broadest sympathies, and highest piety. Her evident unselfishness is beyond worldly understanding. The fragrance of her simple faith is the ultimate in mother love. Here are some factors in her successful motherhood:

- ◆ The baby in her home was wanted, welcomed, and loved.
- ◆ She very early dedicated her child to God.
- ◆ She kept her child in touch with the church.
- ◆ She put spiritual values before all others.

Such parents are our paramount need today. It could be that God is searching now for some consecrated home through which to send His choice leader for our critical times. Is yours such a home? God can help you make it so.

Prayer: *Lord, help me remember that the little things I do for my children have great influence in days to come.*

Where Do They Get It?

Scripture: "He must manage his own family well and see that his children obey him with proper respect."

(1 Tim. 3:4, NIV)

◆ Plan and pray years before they are born, remembering that children are usually like their parents and grandparents.

◆ Teach them to respect parental authority early in life, and they will be more likely to respect divine authority later.

◆ Pray for wisdom that your parental discipline will be neither too severe nor too lax. Teach them the meaning of "No." Punish only in love and with self-discipline.

◆ Conduct regular family devotion time. Make this interesting and rewarding.

◆ Do not do all their praying for them. Children who are old enough to talk to their parents are old enough to talk to God. Encourage children in open self-expressions of prayer in their own way with proper guidance.

◆ Teach them the importance of faithful attendance at worship.

◆ Demonstrate your love to them, especially when it seems that they deserve it the least.

◆ Give them guidance and instruction for Christian conduct at the house of God. Above all, set the example for them yourselves.

◆ Play with your children. Laugh with them, and let them laugh often. If parents must argue, criticize, or complain, hide yourselves.

◆ Answer all questions without showing surprise or embarrassment.

◆ Encourage them to make friends at church rather than with the popular set at school.

◆ Teach them that work is honorable by involving them and yourselves in it.

Prayer: *Lord, help me to set the proper example first. Help me give my children a godly heritage.*

Love Will Be Our Home

Scripture: "Start a boy on the right road, and even in old age he will not leave it."
(Prov. 22:6, NEB)

Three simple ideas help keep the family Christlike:

◆ *Parental harmony.* Pursue the affections you professed before marriage. If you do not *feel* the same romance, *act* as though you were in love, and the feeling will return. Maintain those common courtesies and kindnesses you expressed to each other in your dating days. Show respect for the individual rights of your companion in all things. Display tenderness and consideration for each other. Allow no barriers. Keep communicating. Be transparently honest. Discipline your feelings, thoughts, attitudes, words, time, and money.

◆ *Child discipline.* Begin early to teach your children right and wrong, what is forbidden and what is expected. When correction or discipline is deserved, make it serious enough that the child will understand, but get it over with and forget it. Pray and counsel with each child individually. Teach the basic fundamentals of honesty, courtesy, fair play, and work. Show no favorites, but show plenty of kindness, patience, affection, and appreciation.

◆ *Family prayers.* If your family is not currently praying together, begin today. Mealtime is an ideal opportunity. Before anyone leaves the table, read from the Bible and bow in prayer together. Use a devotional guide appropriate to the age of your family. Encourage scripture memorization. Avoid "preaching" and long prayers; make this an enjoyable, unhurried experience. Let everyone take turns reading and praying. Make family altar time a rewarding habit.

Prayer: *God, make me the balanced, sensible, and godly parent my family needs to see.*

Is There a Non-Christian in the House?

Scripture: "Fathers, do not exasperate your children; instead, bring them up in the training and instruction of the Lord."

(Eph. 6:4, NIV)

All of us want happy homes of unity and Christian love. But often Christian households have non-Christian family members. How should we deal with this?

◆ *Continue to put Christ at the center.* Since He is the Source of all true happiness, do not push Him to the background. Lead your family in reading His Word and praying to Him daily. Take Him into your family conferences. Recognize His presence in every choice and every action.

◆ *Take special care with the non-Christian members of your family.* They may not share your standards of ethics and morals. Remember that coming to Christ cannot be forced. Respect their right to refuse even when you know they are choosing wrongly. Make your walk with Christ so attractive that they will want that relationship. Do more praying for them than they know.

◆ *Recognize that each person in your household is a separate individual regardless of age.* Accept one another without attempting to remake everyone according to your private pattern. Do not be critical if others have likes and dislikes you do not share. Remember that the 12 men whom Christ chose were all different. God chose not to make us all alike.

◆ *Find a common level of fellowship that will include all.* If people within one home have varying religious beliefs, it is all the more important that a common ground of harmony be found. Follow the pattern of the Master who loved all. His love will prevail if it is displayed in simplicity and purity.

Prayer: *Teach us, God, to cut slack where we should, to compromise where needed, and to love always.*

Susanna's Rules

Scripture: "Lo, children are an heritage of the Lord: and the fruit of the womb is his reward."

(Ps. 127:3)

Samuel and Susanna Wesley, parents of John and Charles Wesley, had some definite rules by which their home and their 19 children were regulated. In her book *Susanna*, Rebecca L. Harmon relates some of these:

◆ The children were taught the Lord's prayer as soon as they could speak. They said this prayer regularly at rising and bedtime.

◆ They were taught very early to distinguish the Sabbath from other days.

◆ They were involved daily in family prayers.

◆ They received nothing they cried for and learned to speak kindly for what they wanted.

◆ The parents made it a priority to conquer the children's will and bring them to an obedient temper.

◆ Any child guilty of a fault was not punished if confession and restitution were made.

◆ Everyone learned to respect one another's property.

◆ Promises were sacred and were strictly observed.

◆ A special time was set aside each week for Susanna to spend with each child in education, instruction, and fellowship.

Prayer: *Father, give me wisdom beyond my years to rear the children in my home. Make me a loving parent.*

Serious Family Business

Scripture: "Impress [these commandments] on your children. Talk about them when you sit at home . . . walk along the road . . . lie down and . . . get up."
(Deut. 6:7, NIV)

He farmed more than 600 acres and milked 150 cows twice daily. But his most important work was the spiritual training of his eight children . . . as well as the nourishing of his own soul.

Here was his method. He set his alarm for 4 A.M. and spent 30 minutes in prayer and Bible reading alone with God. His wife did the same thing at the same time in another part of the house.

At 4:30 he called the children together for family worship before breakfast and the work of the day. Family worship was not hurried, nor could it be interrupted. While the eight children and their parents sat in a sizable family circle, the devotional time opened with scripture quotations by all persons present. Memory verses were assigned systematically each Monday morning and memorized by Wednesday. It is surprising how much scripture can be absorbed in 20 years by learning a new verse each week and hearing 10 or 12 other persons quoting their verses.

Following the memory verses, the head of the home would then read a scripture lesson, punctuated by frequent comments from some favorite Bible scholar. At the end of the reading, the entire family would kneel while the father prayed or called on someone else to pray.

Before the noon meal and again before the evening meal, the process was repeated. It may not be the modern way or even the best way to do it, but it was a rewarding way. I know, for I *enjoyed* our family devotions for my first 19 years.

Prayer: *Lord, at least help me to be consistent with a family devotion plan of some kind. Burden me with a hunger to keep it simple and regular.*

An Open Letter to Cynthia Ann

Scripture: "That [Christ] might come to stand first in everything." (Col. 1:18, GOODSPEED)

Years ago this letter was written to my baby granddaughter. Its message is timelessly true.

My Dear Cynthia Ann:

Because you are so young, so eager, so charming, and so full of promise, I thought I would jot down a few New Year's resolutions for your consideration. Maybe you will appreciate them more later on than you do today.

Actually, these are secondhand resolutions. I got them from your great-grandparents. I hope they will have as much meaning for you and give you as much guidance as they have for me.

◆ I will shun the company of questionable people and questionable places.

◆ I will be deaf to verbal smut and garbage.

◆ I will refuse to allow temptations to illicit sex experiences.

◆ I will never try the first cigarette, alcoholic beverage, or drug.

◆ I will give my soul and body to Jesus Christ at His first call.

◆ I will give my money and talents to my church.

◆ I will give my time and efforts in helping others.

◆ I will give my tongue and hands to advance Christ's kingdom.

◆ I will give my mind and thoughts to the study of the Bible and good books.

◆ I will keep my past, present, and future in the hands of my loving Lord.

Although you are only 15 months old this New Year's season, your grandmother and I pray for you daily—as do your parents. In a few shorts years you will be a teenager, making choices you will be too young to make without God's help. But with Christ's help you can do all things, for He will strengthen you.

Prayer: *Father, I desire to place You first in my life by making You first in my affections, possessions, and priorities.*

Finding Faith in
Well-known Characters

Character in the Crucible

Scripture: "You meant to do me harm;
but God meant to bring good."
(Gen. 50:20, NEB)

The life of Joseph reveals steps in building the character that God ultimately used to save His entire chosen people.

◆ *He achieved maturity.* Outgrowing his coat of many colors, he signified his refusal to be spoiled by a doting father. He quit bragging about his dreams involving his own superiority.

◆ *He learned to say YES.* He accepted his troubles in stride. He made the best of every situation—the pit, the murder threat, being sold into slavery, misunderstanding, persecution, character assassination, broken promises, and unjust punishments.

◆ *He learned to say NO.* He refused the temptation to defile himself. He spurned the pleasures of sin even at the price of being jailed. He chose to be true in prison rather than impure in the king's palace.

◆ *He guarded his heart.* He kept all his troubles on the surface, refusing to let them reach down into his heart. He cultivated wholesome attitudes that guided his life.

◆ *He stood tall.* He would not stoop to take advantage of an evil woman. He refused the questionable luxuries of self-pity and retaliation when his friends forgot their promises to open his prison door. He was too big to hold a grudge against his brothers who plotted his murder.

◆ *He cultivated humility and gratitude.* Always prepared for promotion, he never sought it or expected it. Not ashamed of his humble beginnings, he remembered his debt to his family and fulfilled it.

Prayer: *Lord, teach me to grow spiritually so that my character, judgment, and relationships will mature!*

The Best-laid Plans...

Scripture: "But he did not know that the LORD
had left him."

(Judg. 16:20, NIV)

God has a plan for every life. This was certainly true of Samson, for an angel announced to his mother the special blueprints of his life before he was born. From the day of his birth, he was dedicated to the special task of Israel's deliverance. But he made terrible errors that marred God's plan for his life forever.

◆ *He paid much attention to physical strength but little to spiritual strength.* Our emphasis on physical fitness and mental training is well-placed, but above all we need to place our spiritual lives first.

◆ *He associated with the wrong crowd.* He found his friends among God's enemies. Strong as he was, Samson could not bring them up to his level and instead degraded himself to theirs.

◆ *He neglected the discipline of his sex life.* He took his liberties—and became a slave. Samson was bound like a captured beast, and both his eyes were gouged out. Self-discipline would have saved him.

◆ *He talked too much.* He revealed his spiritual secrets to his spiritual enemies. John Wesley believed that no one could talk 30 minutes without saying something he shouldn't.

◆ *He took his relationship with God for granted.* He didn't check up often enough. Too late he discovered that God was gone, and he did not know it.

Prayer: *O Lord, always make me reliant upon You.
Keep me true to Your will.*

Confessions and Regrets

Scripture: "I have sinned . . . I have played the fool,
and have erred exceedingly."

(1 Sam. 26:21)

Saul's commentary at the end of his life revealed a tearful confession.

◆ *He confessed that little sins do not long remain little.* Saul's sinful jealousy may have seemed small in its beginning when the people chanted the victory song after the battle, "Saul hath slain his thousands, and David his ten thousands" (1 Sam. 18:7). But that wrong attitude, that little spirit of wanting all the credit, that small sin of seeking popularity grew to become the all-consuming cancer of his soul. And it destroyed him.

◆ *He confessed that hidden sins do not long remain hidden.* When he spared Agag and the best of the fatted cattle, he hid them away from the prophet of God. But he could not hide them from God! The hidden sin was revealed and so was the hidden motive—selfishness. Covered sin has a way of raising its ugly head at the wrong time.

◆ *He confessed that even God's anointed may be lost.* Who had a better beginning than Saul? He was from sturdy stock. He was every inch a king in appearance, standing head and shoulders above the others. At first he was humble, hardworking, unassuming, and God-fearing. Yet Saul lost his soul, eventually crying out in awful desperation, "God is departed from me, and answereth me no more" (1 Sam. 28:15).

◆ *He confessed that sin has its fearful consequences.* The once great monarch cried out in remorse, "I have sinned . . . I have played the fool, and have erred exceedingly" (1 Sam. 26:21). He fell upon his own sword, a suicide tumbling hopelessly into hell. Unconfessed sin brings everlasting consequences.

Prayer: *O God, make me quick to confess sin and error. Both of these hurt You, me, and others. Cleanse and restore me!*

Repentance Results

Scripture: "Restore to me again the joy of your salvation, and make me willing to obey you."

(Ps. 51:12, TLB)

David's agonizing prayer of bitter confession and repentance is recorded in Ps. 51. It follows closely the discovery of his terrible sin by Nathan (2 Sam. 12). This account contains all of the elements of dramatic human history: temptation, adultery, murder, death, discovery of sin, conviction for sin, repentance, restoration, and consequence.

The focal point of the entire episode occurred when Nathan, guided by the Lord, confronted David and brought him to repentance. David experienced the bitterness of conviction, prompting him to repent and beg for mercy.

Listen to his prayer: "Have mercy upon me . . . blot out my transgressions. Wash me throughly from mine iniquity, and cleanse me from my sin. . . . I acknowledge my transgressions: and my sin is ever before me. . . . Purge me . . . wash me . . . blot out all mine iniquities. Create in me a clean heart . . . Restore unto me the joy of thy salvation . . . Deliver me from bloodguiltiness" (vv. 1-3, 8-10).

This is not the picture of a man carefully kneeling at the altar, arranging the crease in his trousers. It shows the repentant sinner running to God, falling before Him with tears of remorse, confession, repentance, and restitution. God knows the sincere heart. The forgiven stands with tear-stained face upturned and says with assurance: "A broken and a contrite heart, O God, thou wilt not despise" (v. 17). That prayer strikes fire!

Prayer: *Above all else, O God, remind me that I cannot fool You. And should I try, remind me of this psalm.*

Mental Without Moral

Scripture: "Solomon outdid all the kings of the earth in wealth and wisdom" (2 Chron. 9:22, NEB); "The LORD was angry with Solomon because his heart had turned away" (1 Kings 11:9, NEB).

Solomon was called the wisest man who ever lived. Yet it was he who plunged God's chosen people from their greatest splendor into idol worship, beastly corruption, disunity, and ultimate captivity.

Because Solomon's wisdom was a gift from God, he was God-made rather than self-made. With this insight he was able to judge rightly, to strengthen the nation, to build many cities, to write wisdom literature, to build a house of worship, and to gain world fame.

But Solomon did not allow God to have full control of his wisdom. Though he had mental perception, he lacked moral understanding. He was wise but not good. His life reminds us that truth is more than mere intellectual comprehension.

And because Solomon's wisdom was intellectual rather than moral, his foolish heart eclipsed his wise head. He *knew* better than he *did*. His wisdom outran his obedience. His intellectual concepts did not curb his carnal desires. He yielded to his passions rather than God's precepts. His knowledge without obedience was an insult to the God who made him wise—a mockery of the Holy One.

But Solomon's wisdom was powerless to save his soul. Paul observed that "the world by wisdom knew not God." Sadly, Solomon died as he lived—self-centered, lustful, corrupt, greedy, godless, and doomed. Unlike David, he left no repentant Ps. 51. With all his wisdom, he missed the way that even fools may find. And in his sinful foolishness, he plunged an entire nation downward to ruin.

Prayer: Lord, save me from being so mighty that I would consider myself almighty.

After the Victory

Scripture: "But the LORD was not in the fire: and after the fire a still small voice." (1 Kings 19:12)

Christians sometimes have very dark hours. It is easy to lose your way in the darkness. First Kings 19 offers guidance.

◆ *Prepare for an aftermath on the heels of great victory.* Elijah slid from his Mount Carmel conquest to his juniper tree doldrums in a few short hours. We, too, may experience gloom on the heels of glory as our emotions sag.

◆ *Pay attention to the physical as well as the spiritual.* God provided Elijah with the first "angel food cake" on record—right under the juniper tree (vv. 5-8). Even the strongest Christians cannot afford to ignore the laws of health. Discouragement and despair often come with hunger, weariness, and illness.

◆ *Avoid the superspiritual stance.* Twice Elijah bragged about his jealousy for the Lord's work (vv. 10 and 14) and that he was the only one around with good religion. The superspiritual have blind spots, and spiritual superiority can quickly sidetrack us.

◆ *Do not be swept by the spectacular.* Elijah was impressed by the wind, the earthquake, and the fire, but he discovered that God was also in the "still small voice" (vv. 11-12). The great prophet who had prayed down rain when there had been no rain for 36 months and who had called down fire from heaven on a wet sacrifice now had to settle for a "still small voice." God is the God of the insignificant as well as the spectacular.

◆ *Avoid excessive slumps in the emotional life.* Elijah, man of the mountain-peak victories, was now crawling in a cave (vv. 9, 13). Christians cannot always stand on the high places, but neither can we live too long in the caves of discouragement and darkness. Crawl out into God's sunshine! Look to Him for your balance and perspective.

Prayer: *Lord, when dark times come to my life, remind me to listen and obey Your quiet prompting.*

Can You Pass the Test?

Scripture: "In all of this, Job did not sin or revile God."
(Job 1:22, TLB)

The periods of Job's life can be identified as a series of tests. *The test of prosperity* was the first. He had all that anyone could desire: lovely wife, fine children, nice home, lands, crops, and livestock by the thousands. He was a man of vast wealth, yet he did not let his riches rot his soul. Prosperity is always a test.

The test of adversity fell without warning upon Job. In a tragic moment he lost everything: sheep, oxen, camels, crops, and children! Ten fresh graves hauntingly reminded him of happy, prosperous days, now vanished like a dream. But Job passed this test saying, "The LORD gave, and the LORD hath taken away; blessed be the name of the LORD" (Job 1:21).

Next came *the test of physical affliction.* Job lost his health with what may have been an Asian leprosy. He could not begin again. There was no money for physicians. There was no cure. Covered with sores, he sat on the ground beside the 10 new graves. Yet Job kept his faith in God.

Job's bitterest test may have been *the test of domestic discord.* His wife turned against him and against God. She reasoned: Could Job believe in a God who had let all this happen to him? "Curse God and die," she screamed scornfully in her sin of lost faith. Job was alone, suffering, and dying. The wife of his youthful and prosperous days had left him when his money was gone, his health had disappeared, and his children were dead. Yet Job kept his faith even when he could not understand.

Finally Job endured *the spiritual test.* The "church" turned against Job and sent a committee of three to check up on him. Their harsh and unanswerable questions brought him to the brink of despair. They stabbed his soul with the dagger of doubt.

In all of this, Job refused to deny his faith in God. God brought him through. He will do the same for you today.

Prayer: *Lord, when life throws its curves, help me to remain faithful and not resent You.*

Fatal Fallacies

Scripture: "I can *never* be lost to your Spirit! I can *never* get away from my God." (Ps. 139:7, TLB)

Jonah, star of children's favorite Bible story, made serious adult errors in judgment and spiritual discernment.

◆ *God can get along just fine without me.* Jonah was mistaken. God needed him. There was work to do—people who had never heard God's message. God's work can be limited without us.

◆ *Someone else will do my work if I don't.* Wrong again. Nineveh was lost, and Jonah was appointed messenger. God has a work for each of us to do.

◆ *It is possible to escape God.* Ps. 139 tells us we can never get away from God. Jonah thought he could run away, but there is no hiding place. God is eternally inescapable.

◆ *Running from God silences His call.* This is erroneous. When Jonah discovered he could not escape God, he was refaced with God's call. After the experience with the whale, the call of God came the second time (3:1-2). We can disobey God, but we cannot escape His call.

◆ *God should not be merciful to repenting souls.* Jonah was angry because his preaching brought a merciful revival to Nineveh instead of a mighty destruction from God. There are people who insist that God is not severe enough with the repentant. We must leave God's mercy and justice to His sovereignty.

◆ *The temporal is better than the spiritual.* Are gourds really better than souls, Jonah? You were "exceeding glad [for] the gourd" (4:6), but you did not rejoice for the Nineveh revival. Whatever gives us pleasure reveals much about our spiritual condition.

◆ *God's work can be done without love.* Not so. Jonah failed because he was low on love. He was driven only by force, fear, and duty. Passion for people is God's way.

Prayer: *Save me, Lord, from running from You like Jonah! Teach me to trust You and rest in Your love.*

Passion That Outshines Celebrities

Scripture: "Then [Andrew] brought [Simon] to Jesus."
(John 1:42, NIV)

As far as we know, Andrew never preached a sermon. There is no Epistle of Andrew or Gospel According to Andrew to be found. If he ever wrote anything, we do not have it. If Andrew ever performed a miracle with God's help, no one reported it. What was his trouble? Did Peter and Matthew and John simply outshine him? Was Andrew a failure for God?

Hardly! Although Andrew was no preacher of reputation, one of his converts, Simon Peter, preached a sermon at Pentecost, which resulted in 3,000 converts. So Andrew had a share in these victories. While Andrew wrote no books of the Bible, one of his converts, Simon Peter, was the author of two Epistles in the New Testament. So Andrew will enjoy some of this harvest with Peter. And while Andrew performed no miracle, he introduced a boy to Jesus who multiplied his lunch to feed 5,000 people. Andrew shares in the miracle's blessing!

Andrew did not fail. On the contrary, God's work could have suffered without him and people like him.

Although he was the first of Christ's 12 chosen, Andrew was no ecclesiastical celebrity. He was an ordinary man with an extraordinary passion to introduce others to Jesus. He started at home with his own brother and reached out to others, like the boy with the lunch and the Greeks with their philosophies.

May God give us more Andrews who have a passion for bringing others to Him.

Prayer: *God, fill me with renewed passion for the lost all around me, beginning at home!*

The Price Tag

Scripture: "There was a man called . . . Zaccheus . . . and he was rich."

(Luke 19:2, NASB)

Tremendous similarities exist between Zacchaeus and the rich, young ruler. Both were wealthy. The one earned his money by questionable integrity, while the other must have inherited his riches.

Despite their comfortable lifestyle, Zacchaeus and the rich, young ruler were both unhappy. Their fame, culture, and talents were not enough. Eagerly they sought for something more to satisfy their hearts.

Both men came to Jesus Christ, earnestly, as a thirsty traveler comes to a sparkling spring. Zacchaeus, a short man, ran ahead of the throng and climbed a tree to see Jesus. The rich, young ruler, princely though he was, came running and knelt before Christ, asking sincerely how to attain eternal life. The first brought his badness to Jesus; the second brought his goodness.

Zacchaeus and the rich, young ruler faced the same test—money. Christ put His finger on the root of sin in both lives—selfishness. That root can grow many branches—greed, pride, lust, envy, laziness, habits, and love of money. But when a person sincerely faces Christ, the main root emerges.

Here the similarities of the two men end. Zacchaeus and the rich, young ruler went separate directions. The first said a grand yes to Christ, making solid restitution and utterly obeying Him. The other said a sad no to Christ, saving his money but losing his soul.

Christ is before you today! The choice is yours. The two worlds of eternity await your answer. Choose Christ!

Prayer: *Lord, teach me that my soul is more valuable than my money.*

Forgiven

Scripture: "I tell you, her many sins have been forgiven—for she loved much. But he who has been forgiven little loves little."

(Luke 7:47, NIV)

Our Lord's dealings with a sinful woman (Luke 7:36-50) show us six steps to His forgiving grace.

◆ *Awareness of sin.* Luke said she was a sinner. The Pharisees said it. And Jesus said it. But she was most aware of it, and she didn't try to hide it. The person who will not admit a sinful condition can never be forgiven.

◆ *Remorse.* She came to the feet of Jesus and wept for her sins. Some frown on public confession. They say, "Away with display. Only believe. Only decide for Christ." But not so with this woman. She was remorseful, regretful, and deeply sorry for her sins. This is God's way to forgiveness. Remorse and repentance pave the way for forgiveness.

◆ *Humility.* She humbled herself. She washed His feet with her tears and wiped them with her hair. There was no pride here, no reluctance to kneel, bow low, and admit her need.

◆ *Emotion.* Her feelings were involved when she came face-to-face with her sins and her Savior. She wept in front of skeptical disciples and self-righteous Pharisees. Emotional repentance usually paves the way for forgiveness. Religion must be more than theory; it must be experienced and personal.

◆ *Adoration.* Here is a hidden step to forgiveness. Simon, the host, had not bathed our Lord's feet, had not anointed Him with oil, and had not greeted Him with a welcome kiss. But she bathed His feet with her salty tears, kissed them, and anointed them with her own perfume at a great sacrifice. She expressed her adoration and love in her quest for forgiveness.

◆ *Faith*. Having come this far, it was easy and simple to trust her Savior for forgiveness. She was saved and departed in peace. Forgiveness always brings peace.

> **Prayer:** *Lord, may I always seek to love You in a way that resembles the extent of Your forgiveness of me.*

The Job No One Wants

Scripture: "And fixing their gaze on him, all . . . saw his face like the face of an angel."

(Acts 6:15, NASB)

It takes a special kind of person to be a good martyr for Jesus Christ. Note the qualities of Stephen pictured in Acts 6—7.

◆ *He was full of faith* (6:8). He believed in Christ enough to live for Him or die for Him.

◆ *He was full of power* (6:8). God worked miracles through him. People were affected by God's power in him.

◆ *He had spiritual wisdom* (6:10). He was able to discern. He knew God's Word, much of it by memory. He applied it with wisdom.

◆ *He had an irresistible spirit about him* (6:10). God's Spirit worked through his spirit, and people could not avoid that.

◆ *He faced his enemies with the face of an angel* (6:15). He had lived in contact with God so much that it shone through on his face.

◆ *He fearlessly condemned people for their sins* (7:51). He pointed them out openly.

◆ *He charged them with the murder of Jesus* (7:52). He could have compromised to save himself, but he didn't.

◆ *His message cut its way into their hearts* (7:54). Truth backed up by the Spirit of God always convicts men of sin.

◆ *He was filled with the Holy Spirit* (7:55). No man can be effective in life or in death without this fullness.

◆ *He had an up-to-the-minute contact with heaven* (7:55). Jesus stood to welcome the first martyr.

◆ *He forgave those who killed him* (7:60). He loved his enemies and prayed for those who were stoning him to death.

◆ *His victorious death affected his enemies.* Likely this scene hounded Saul (7:58) all the way to his Damascus road surrender.

Prayer: *O God, when I endure mistreatment, may even my countenance reflect the Spirit of Jesus Christ.*

Spotlight or Shadow?

Scripture: "Paul chose Silas."
(Acts 15:40, NASB)

Some people stand tall—physically and socially. They are head and shoulders above everyone else. Their entire lives are a series of parades and awards. And they keep growing taller even after death.

But these spotlight people cast a shadow, and a few lesser characters are sometimes known simply because they were standing in that shadow of fame. We remember them not because of their own achievements but because they were near someone who achieved. What would we know of Lot if he had not lived in the shadow of Abraham? Or of Aaron except for Moses? This is not to say that lesser people were inferior. Their own lives were simply eclipsed by someone else's greatness. They are the second-chair violinists in life's sprawling symphony.

Silas was a shadows man. He did not choose Paul. Paul chose him—and as a second choice, at that. Silas did not make the decisions; Paul made them. Nor did Silas do much of the preaching; Paul did it. Paul also wrote the Epistles and planned the missionary journey. Paul even got top billing, Luke always referred to the team as "Paul and Silas," not "Silas and Paul." Whether Silas shared in the glory or the prison, it was all because he followed Paul there.

Silas is to be commended, however, for not chafing in the shadows—for submitting without irritation to the eccentricities, popularities, and punishments of Paul. And surely Silas will share more abundantly in the glories of the taller saint in whose shadow he served on earth. Often it takes more grace to be sweet in the shadows than in the sunshine.

Prayer: *O Lord, remind me that my worth is in You and Your love for me, not merely how I rank in the eyes of others!*

Basin and Towel Living

Scripture: "I commend to you our sister Phoebe,
who is a servant of the church."

(Rom. 16:1, NASB)

Tradition tells us that a woman named Phoebe had the responsibility of carrying Paul's manuscript of the Book of Romans from Corinth to Rome. Who was this woman so trusted by Paul, the man who told women to keep silent in the church? Two verses tell us all we need to know (Rom. 16:1-2).

She was a "servant of the church": not a paid member of the staff, not a full-time employee, not a part-time worker, but a *servant* of the church. If she had talent as a soloist or musician, Paul didn't say so. If she had money or influence, Paul forgot to tell us.

But she was a *servant* of the church. Elected or not, she served. Appreciated or not, she served. Appointed or not, she served. Having her own way or not, she served.

She got the title of "servant of the church" not by influence, but by willingness; not by money, but by dependability; not by being easily offended, but by always being gracious; not by putting herself forward, but by humility; not by place-seeking, but by unselfishness; not by getting attention, but by giving unrewarded service; not by climbing the ladder of popularity, but by gladly performing the unglamorous tasks shunned by others; not by waiting for promotion to an outstanding position, but by serving even when no one else noticed.

Dependable Christians always serve this way. Our Lord set the pattern by saying, "I am among you as he that serveth" (Luke 22:27).

Prayer: *Lord, regardless of honors, applause, or recognition, help me remember that my highest calling is to be a servant!*